GW00467565

SOUTH COAST RAILWAYS ~

WORTHING

TO

CHICHESTER

Vic Mitchell and Keith Smith

Other Sussex railway books by the same authors,
from Middleton Press, at the same price–

Branch Lines to Midhurst
Branch Lines to Horsham
Branch Line to Selsey
South Coast Railways—
Brighton to Worthing

First published 1983
Cover design—Deborah Mitchell
ISBN 0 906520 06 1

© *Middleton Press, 1983*

Published by Middleton Press
Easebourne Lane
Midhurst, West Sussex.
GU29 9AZ

Printed & bound by Biddles Ltd.,
Guildford and Kings Lynn.

INDEX

MAPS

Except where otherwise stated, the scale is 25″ to 1 mile but the following initial letters apply throughout.

BM   Bench Mark
Cr   Crane
MP   Mile Post
SB   Signal Box
SP   Signal Post

ACKNOWLEDGEMENTS

We would like to thank the editor of the *Railway Magazine* for the use of the maps in the introduction and the East Sussex County Library for permission to use photographs from the Madgwick collection. We would like to record our appreciation of the help received from the photographers named in the captions and also from: Worthing Reference Library, Littlehampton Museum, G. Croughton, P. Jerrome, C. Durrant, J. Edgington, D. Elleray, Miss S. Endacott, R. Harmer, J.H. Knight, N. Langridge, C. Packham, D. Osborne, E.W. Pratt, R. Randell, R.C. Riley, N. Stanyon, Mrs. E.M. Wallis and D. Wallis. Our thanks also go to M. Grainger, A.G. Richards and H.S.F. Thompson for their darkroom skills. As ever our gratitude is immeasurable for our patient wives.

GEOGRAPHICAL SETTING

The coastal plain is at its widest in the Chichester area and tapers to a point at Brighton. Since the railway from Worthing to Chichester runs almost straight across the middle of the plain, little civil engineering work was required and most roads could cross it on the level. Early railway builders were required to provide very few road bridges, unlike the engineers of lines from the 1860s onwards. It is paradoxical that most of the early lines remain open today with their numerous level crossings delaying road traffic, whilst most of the later lines are now closed, leaving redundant bridges (some still owned by BR) to impede traffic flow.

The gap cut through the South Downs by the River Arun had given the railway promoters a relatively easy route for the so-called Mid-Sussex line through Pulborough and Arundel. Conversely the Arun gave the engineers of the coast line a headache, as they had to provide a movable bridge to carry the line over it, since coastal shipping still went upstream as far as Arundel where the first road bridge was situated.

HISTORICAL BACKGROUND

The first passenger carrying railway in Sussex was opened between Brighton and Shoreham on 12th May 1840, over a year before the line to London was completed. Building a single track along the coast first facilitated the construction of the southern part of the route to London, as materials could be brought in by sea via Shoreham harbour. The track was doubled before services were extended to Worthing on 24th November 1845. For the next 50 years or more there was much public agitation for a direct line northwards from Worthing to London, but this was never to be. Westward extension was made to Lyminster on 16th March and to Chichester on 8th June of the following year, Portsmouth being reached in 1847.

The Horsham branch from Three Bridges was extended to Petworth in 1859, but it was not until 3rd August 1863 that the link between Pulborough and Ford via Arundel was opened. A branch to Littlehampton was brought into use two weeks later and one to Bognor on 1st June the following year.

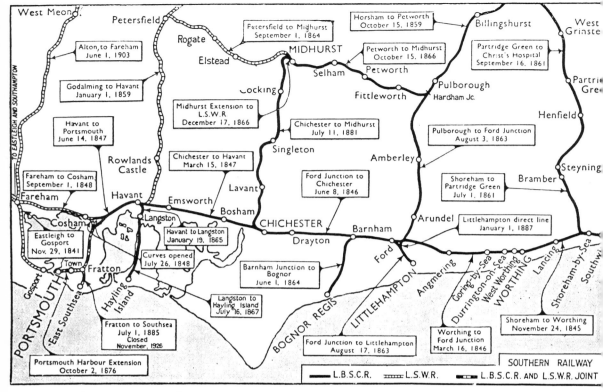

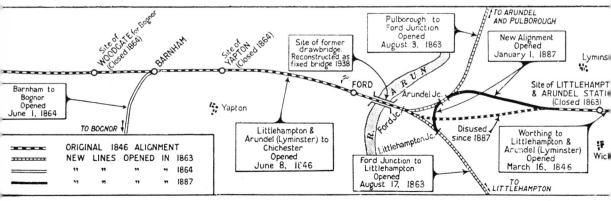

Chronological map showing the development of the West Coast section of the former L.B.S.C.R.

Until the opening of separate stations at Arundel and Littlehampton, a station of that name was provided on the main coast line at the point at which the road between the two towns crossed it, near Lyminster.

In 1887, the junction of the Little-hampton branch was rearranged, as shown on the accompanying plan. In the same year, plans were made for an electric tramway, 1 mile long, from Littlehampton station to the seafront, but it was never built.

On 4th November 1889, a new station was opened at West Worthing to serve the developing residential area in the parish of

Sketch plan (not to scale) of the present and past railway alignments in the neighbourhood of Ford.

Heene. Unfortunately, hopes of continued rapid growth at West Worthing did not materialise, and in 1893 financial difficulties intervened and development came temporarily to a standstill. In the same year, the progress of the town was still further retarded by the disastrous typhoid epidemic, which caused a serious financial loss to the railway. It was said that in the month of August there was not a single visitor in Worthing, and it was several years before the town fully recovered from these set-backs.

1898 saw the directors of the Selsey Tramway proposing the construction of a similar light railway between Worthing and Horsham, via Findon, but funds were not forthcoming.

During World War I, a branch was laid south from Ford station to serve the airfield. It was operated by a small industrial-type tank locomotive for about 2 years. In 1920, a Light Railway Order was sought by Col. H.F. Stephens (Engineer of the Selsey Tramway and numerous other minor railways in Britain) for the construction of a railway on a similar route, terminating at Climping at a point 300 yds. west of Littlehampton swing bridge.

ACCIDENTS

Unlike the relatively trouble free line from Brighton to Worthing, the section covered by this album has been most unlucky.

Apart from collisions with level crossing gates, the first accident appears to have occurred on 30th September 1847, when the guard of a train hit his head on an overbridge near Angmering whilst attending to luggage which was being carried on the carriage roof, stage-coach style.

A disaster occurred on 27th November 1851, when the 10 p.m. train from Brighton over-ran the signals at the approach to the single track Arun bridge and collided with a goods train which had almost crossed the bridge. The fireman died and the driver immediately set about ending his own life, first by attempting to cut his throat and then by jumping in the river. Both failed.

On 4th August 1920, a DI tank engine crashed through the buffers at Littlehampton owing to an error in connecting the brake hoses.

The driver of a train from Brighton was killed when it ran past signals at Ford, on 5th August 1951, and collided with the rear of a Bognor train standing in the loop. There were 47 injuries.

Cottages at Littlehampton were nearly demolished when K class no. 32339 became derailed on 28th April 1953.

On 8th February 1962, a forgetful signalman at Drayton allowed a train from Portsmouth to run into the back of the previous one, causing 17 injuries.

During Goodwood Race week in 1962, chaos was caused when a 6-coach train from Brighton to Portsmouth was derailed whilst entering Barnham station. The enquiry revealed that a loose washer in the electrical equipment controlling the points caused them to move when the train was part way over them.

Again there were many injuries when a train from Brighton ran into a Southdown bus on Roundstone level crossing, near Angmering, on 23rd September 1965. This again was due to a signalman's error.

In March 1983, a derailed freight wagon damaged 2½ miles of the up track between Chichester and Barnham before being detected, but there were no injuries.

PASSENGER SERVICES

Upon opening, the coast line was provided with seven trains each way on weekdays and three on Sundays. Owing to the harsh economic climate of 1849, the weekday service was reduced to five return journeys, but directors felt that the Sunday service could not be pruned. By 1861, the frequency had been restored to seven trains, which was increased to nine by 1890, there still being only three on Sundays. Bognor and Littlehampton were served by branch line trains from Barnham and Ford Junctions respectively.

By 1869, the Mid-Sussex line was carrying six passenger trains each way, although one down train divided at Three Bridges to form fast and stopping portions.

No. 00322   **1/F**

THE PULLMAN CAR COMPANY LTD.
and
THE SOUTHERN RAILWAY COMPANY

LONDON to BRIGHTON, HOVE   BRIGHTON, HOVE, EASTBOURNE
EASTBOURNE, WORTHING   BOGNOR REGIS, ANGMERING
WEST WORTHING, ANGMERING   WEST WORTHING
or BOGNOR REGIS   or WORTHING to LONDON

2/-

Good for one trip only in either direction when accompanied by a First-Class Railway Season
Ticket and subject to seats being available in the Pullman Cars.

SEE OTHER CONDITIONS AT BACK   *BY ORDER*

The 1890 timetable showed eleven direct London trains, three of which divided at Horsham to give a fast portion to Portsmouth and a stopping train to Bognor via Littlehampton. The 4.55 from London Bridge was shown as first stop Chichester, a feature that would be welcomed by some of today's travellers.

In 1910, the 6.25 am from Brighton is shown terminating at Chichester where it waited for over an hour before proceeding to Victoria via Midhurst. For the rest of the day the coast was served by 12 trains starting alternately from Victoria and Brighton. The early evening brought more variety, with London Bridge departures at 4.50 (calling only at Arundel and Chichester but slipping coaches for Bognor whilst passing non-stop through Barnham at 6.21) and at 5.8, which was an all Pullman train to Bognor calling at Worthing and West Worthing. The GWR was one of the few other companies using slip coaches to any extent at that time.

In 1905, a "Motor Train" service was introduced between Brighton and Worthing with some journeys extended to West Worthing. This consisted of one coach coupled to a small tank engine, initially a Terrier class, and fitted with driving controls at the end of the coach so that it could be propelled on the return journey. This additional local service was so successful that it was extended to Littlehampton in 1907; increased to two coaches and in some cases four (two each side of the engine).

The first regular service to the West started in 1908 and was to Plymouth, but was short lived. In 1922, regular running to Cardiff started, once a day, and later similar services to Bournemouth and Plymouth were introduced.

Electrification between London, Brighton and West Worthing on 1st January 1933 introduced a regular interval service on the coast line for the first time. Extension of the conductor rail to Portsmouth, the Mid-Sussex line and the branches enabled a similar service to be worked on these lines in 1938. War time disrupted routine but by 1948 the basic number of trains per hour was as follows – 3 Brighton - West Worthing (all stations and halts), 2 Brighton - Littlehampton (one of which was extended to Bognor), 1 Brighton - Portsmouth Harbour. On the Mid-Sussex line there were 2 stopping trains per hour to Littlehampton (one ran on to Bognor) and an hourly service from Victoria, which split at Barnham for Bognor and Portsmouth, running alternate hours via Three Bridges or Dorking. As now, an hourly train from Littlehampton to Victoria called at all stations to Worthing, then Shoreham and Hove, avoiding Brighton by use of the Preston Park spur.

Various combinations of these services have been operated in the ensuing years but at a steadily reducing frequency. A notable exception was the short lived shuttle service between Littlehampton and Arundel bay platform, connecting with London trains. Since May 1978, most Mid-Sussex line trains have called at Gatwick Airport.

Changes and recent improvements in the through trains to the west are discussed in our companion album on the Brighton to Worthing line, but since its publication further improvements were made in May 1983. These include a through train to Penzance on Fridays with a Saturday train to Plymouth extended to Penzance in the summer (despite a misprint in the time-table). There are also through trains to Cardiff and Bristol on Sundays from Brighton. The expansion of these cross country services, and also those to the Midlands and North from Brighton and Portsmouth, have brought greater comfort and convenience to the passenger, at the same time adding operating interest for the railway observer.

September 1953

First and Third Class Ordinary Single Fares
FROM AND TO LONDON
(VICTORIA AND LONDON BRIDGE)

STATION	ROUTE	ORDINARY SINGLE *	
		1st Class	3rd Class
		s. d.	s. d.
ARUNDEL ...	Via Horsham	12/9	8/6
BOGNOR REGIS	Via Horsham†	14/9	9/10
CHICHESTER ...	Via Horsham†	14/9	9/10
HAVANT	Via Horsham†	14/9	9/10
LITTLEHAMPTON ...	Via Horsham or Brighton or Preston Spur	13/8	9/1
PORTSMOUTH & SOUTHSEA	Via Horsham†	16/3	10/10
PORTSMOUTH HARBOUR ...	Via Horsham†	16/6	11/-
COWES	Via Horsham, Portsmouth and Ryde Pier Head	21/7	15/1
NEWPORT ...		20/9	14/6
RYDE ESPLANADE ...		18/7	13/1
SANDOWN ...		19/10	13/11
SHANKLIN ...		20/4	14/3
VENTNOR ...		21/4	14/11
FRESHWATER ...	Via Horsham, Portsmouth, Ryde, Newport & Southern Vectis Bus	22/5½	16/2½
YARMOUTH ...		21/10½	15/7½

Children 3 and under 14 years, half-fare.

* Return fares are double the single journey charge (with certain exceptions).
†Slightly higher fares apply via Brighton or Preston Spur.

Availability of Tickets

Single — Three days (Sunday a dies non except when issued on that day).

Return —Outward and return halves valid for three months from date shown thereon.

Tickets from London can be purchased in advance at any London or Suburban Station.

Where cheques or postal orders for the purchase of tickets are remitted by post, they should be made payable to the Railway Executive.

For any further Information respecting Excursions and Cheap Tickets, or in regard to travel facilities generally, application should be made to this Region's Offices and Agencies, or to the Commercial Superintendent, British Railways, Southern Region, Waterloo Station, S.E.I. (Telephone: Waterloo 5100.)

THE SOUTH COAST AND LONDON

Week Days—*Continued.*

	aft	aft	aft	aft	aft	mrn	aft	aft	aft	aft	aft	aft	aft	mrn	aft	aft	mrn	aft	aft	aft	aft	aft	aft	aft	aft	aft	aft	aft	aft	aft
370 Yarmouth ......dep.						10SO55								11SX32			11SX32												Through Train, Bognor Regis and Littlehampton to London Bridge.	
370 Cowes ...... "						11SO20								12 25			12SX26													
370 Newport ...... "						12SO3								12 36			12SX37													
370 Ventnor ...... "						11SO55								12 v 20			12SX40													
370 Shanklin ...... "						12SO7								12 v 32			12SX52													
370 Sandown ...... "						11SO59								12 v 39			1SX1													
525 Ryde Pier (Boat).. "						12SO50								1 20			1SX35													
Portsmouth Harbour..dep.						1 53								2 10			2 23													
Portsmouth & Southsea "	1 42					1 57								2 14			2 27													
Fratton	1 45					2 0								2 16			2 30													
Bedhampton Halt	1 53																													
Havant 246	1 55					2 9								2 25			2 39													
Warblington Halt	1 57			Saturdays only.										2 27																
Emsworth	2 0					—								2 30																
Southbourne Halt	2 3					—								2 33																
Nutbourne Halt	2 5					—								2 36																
Bosham	2 9													2 39																
Fishbourne Halt	2 12													2 42																
Chichester Y	2 15					2 22								2 46			2 54													
Barnham ......arr.						2 31								2 55			3 3													
Bognor Regis arr.	Stop					2 51								3 11			3 11													
Bognor Regis dep.		2 10		2 22		2 10					2 30		2 44	2 44			2 55												3 5	
Barnham ......dep.		2 16				2 31					2 36		2 51	2 56			3 5													
Ford (Sussex)		2 21		R							2 41		2 56				R												R	
Littlehampton arr.	aft	2 25		2 36		2 46					2 46		3 0				3 25							P					3 17	
Littlehampton dep.	2 36	2 28		2 41		2 9				2 56	2 49	2 59	3 3				3 3							3 9		3 16			3 21	
Ford (Sussex) ......arr.	2 40									3 0																3 21				
Angmering Y	Stop			Through Train, Bognor Regis and Littlehampton to Victoria.							2 58			3 6	Saturdays only.		Through Train, Bognor Regis to Victoria							3 19		Stop				
Goring-by-Sea											3 3			3 11										3 24						
Durrington-on-Sea	aft										3 5													3 27						
West Worthing U	2 38								2 50		3 7			3 14		3 20								3 30				3 38		
Worthing Central	2 40					2 48			2 52		3 9			3 17		3 22								3 34				3 40	Saturdays only.	
Ham Bridge Halt N									2 55							3 24														
Lancing	2 44								2 58		3 13					3 27												3 41		
Shoreham Airport L	2 46								3 0							3 30														
Shoreham-by-Sea K 215	2 49					2 55			3 3		3 17			3 25	3 28	3 32								3 40				3 48		
Southwick	2 52								3 6		3 21					3 35												3 51		
Fishersgate Halt									3 9							3 38														
Portslade and West Hove	2 55								3 11		3 24					3 40												3 54		
Aldrington Halt 246									3 14		3 27					3 43												3 57		
Hove	2 59					3 3			3 16		3 29			3 33	3 36	3 45								3 50				3 59		
Holland Road Halt									3 18							3 47														
Brighton (below) ......arr.	3 2					3 6			3 20		3 32			3 36	3 41	3 50												4 2		
Arundel	Stop	2 35		2 49		Stop			Stop			3 5	3 10	Stop		Stop	3 14							Through Train Littlehampton to Victoria.					3 28	
Amberley		2 40										3 10																		
Pulborough J 244		2 48										3 18																		
Billingshurst ....(Horsham		2 55										3 25					3 25												3 40	
Christ's Hospital, West		3 2										3 32																		
Horsham 245, 425 arr.		3 6		3 13								3 37					3 42		Saturdays excepted.										3 56	
Horsham 245, 425 dep.		Stop		3 14								Stop																		
Dorking North H 425				3 32																										
Sutton 257, 289, 309 arr.				3 49														aft												
Horsham ......dep.					3 17												3 43	3 47											3 58	
Littlehaven Halt					3 19													3 50												
Fay Gate					3 23													3 54												
Ifield					3 28													3 58												
Crawley ......(234	aft				3 31													4 1												
Three Bridges (below)..arr.	P				3 34												3 55	4 5									P			
Ore ......dep.	2SX0				Stop		2 25	2 13										Stop	2 30						2 42		3 0			
Hastings	2SX5						2 31	2 16											2 35						2 45		3 5			
St. Leonards (W.S.)	2SX8						2 34	2 18						Saturdays only.					2 38						2 47		3 8			
" (W.M.)								2 20											2 40						2 49					
Bexhill (Central) G	2SX15						2 42	2 25											2 46						2 54		3 15			
Collington Halt								2 28																	2 57					
Cooden Beach	2SX19						2 46	2 31											2 50						3 0		3 19			
Norman's Bay Halt								2 34																	3 3					
Pevensey Bay Halt								2 38																	3 7					
Pevensey and Westham							2 53	2 40											2 56	Saturdays only.					3 9					
Hampden Park F								2 45								P			3 2						3 15					
Eastbourne arr.	2SX32							2 49	aft							aft			3 6						3 19	aft	3 32			
Eastbourne dep.	2 36						Sats. only.	2 52	2f57							3 10			3 10						3 22	3 27	3 36			3 39
Hampden Park F								2 55	3f0										3 13						3 25	3 30				3 43
Polegate 239								2 59	Stop										3 17						3 29					3 48
Berwick								3 5																	3 35					Stop
Glynde								3 11																	3 41					
Lewes 239 ......arr.	2 56	aft					3 13	3 16						aft					3 33						3 46		3 56			aft
Seaford ......dep.	2 37	2 47						3 mins later on Sats.						3 5		Saturdays only.			3 14	3 14		3SX24	Saturdays excepted.				3 37			3 44
Bishopstone Halt	2 40	2 50																	3 17	3 17		3SX27					3 40			3 47
Newhaven Harbour	2 42	2 52												3 11					3 19	3 19		3SX29					3 42			3 49
" Town	2 44	2 54												3 14					3 21	3 21		3SX31					3 44			3 51
Southease & Rodmell Halt		2 59																	3 26	3 26		3SX36								3 56
Lewes 239 ......arr.	2 53	3 4	aft											3 24					3 31	3 31		3SX41					3 53			4 1
Lewes ......dep.		3 5	3 11					3 17												3 32			3 37		3 47					4 2
Falmer		3 12						3 24												3 39			3 44		3 54					4 9
London Road (Brighton)		3 16						3 29												3 43			3 48		3 58					4 13
Brighton ......arr.		3 19	3 27					3 31												3 46			3 51		4 1					4 16
Lewes ......dep.	2 57						3 14	Stop						3 25					3 35			3 42	Stop				3 57			
Cooksbridge																						3 47								
Plumpton																						3 52								
Wivelsfield (below)																						3 58	Saturdays only. Not after 10th Sept.							
Haywards Heath ...arr.	3 14				aft	aft		aft	aft									aft	3 54		aft	4 3					4 14			
Brighton ......dep.					2 58	3 8		3 18	3 25									3 28			3 38									
Preston Park					3 1	3 11												3 31			3 41									
Hassocks D					3 9			Saturdays only. 30th July to 10th Sept.										3 39												
Burgess Hill					3 13													3 43												
Wivelsfield (above)					3 15													3 45												
Haywards Heath C arr.					3 21	3 26						aft						3 52			4 0			4 8						
Haywards Heath C dep.	3 15				3 21	3 26						3 35						3 52	3 55		4 0	4 6		4 8			4 14			
Ardingly												3 40										4 10								
Horsted Keynes 239. arr.	P			R					P			3 46				P	R					4 14		P			P		R	
Balcombe					3 27													3 58												
Three Bridges (above)					3 37												3 56	4 7			4 12									
Gatwick Airport				Saturdays only.	3 41	3 39	Saturdays only.											4 11												
Horley					3 44													4 14	Saturdays excepted		4 18								Saturdays only.	
Salfords					3 48													4 18												
Earlswood					3 52													4 22					aft							
Redhill 274					3 58	3 50											4 9	4 29					4 18							
Merstham					4 2													4 33												
Coulsdon South					4 8													4 39												
Purley ......(309					4 12													4 43					4 33							
East Croydon 234, 289, arr.	3 45				4 17	4 4	4 1	4 7						4 15		4 20	4 23	4 48	4 30		4 37		4 39	4 41			4 45		4 32	
Norwood Junction B arr.	3*39				4 22	4*18	4*18	4*18								4*36	4*35		4*42		4 42		4 45						4 37	
New Cross Gate ... "																			4*50		4 50		4 57							
LONDON BRIDGE ... "	4*11			4†38	4 36	4*31	4*31	4*31								4*49	4*49	5SX3	4*55		4 55			5*f3			5*f3		4 52	
Clapham Junction A ..arr.						4 16												5SO2	4 45											
VICTORIA ...... "	4 2			4 10	4*40	4 22	4 17	4 28	4 25					4 32		4 36	4 40	5SO7	4 50		4*57			4 57			5 1		4*57	

f 8 mins. later on Sats. † 4 mins. *earlier* on Sats. P Pullman Car facilities available. R Restaurant Car facilities available from Bognor Regis.
SO Saturdays only. SX Saturdays excepted. *v* 5 minutes *earlier* on Saturdays. * Change at East Croydon. † Change at Sutton.

For Other Notes, see page 233; for Continuation of Trains, pages 210 to 233; for Return Journey, pages 158 to 195

A sample hour in the Southern Railway timetable for the summer of 1938.

RAIL MOTOR SERVICES
BRIGHTON, WORTHING AND LITTLEHAMPTON,
AND
BRIGHTON and THE DYKE

DOWN.   **WEEK DAYS.**

		a.m.	a.m.	a.m.	a.m.	July a.m.	a.m.		1 2 3 a.m.	a.m.	a.m.	a.m.		a.m.	noon	July p.m.	p.m.		p.m.		p.m.	July p.m.	p.m.
ghton	dep.	4 55	5 39	6 35	8 0	9 10	9 10		9 15	10 0	10 38	...		11 0	12 0	12 40	12 55		...		1 0	2 20	2 23
nd Road Halt	,,	4 58	5 42	6 39	8 3	9 13	9 13			10 3	10 41	...		11 3	12 3	12 43	12 58				1 3	2 23	2 23
e Junction Halt	,,	5 1	5 45	6 41	8 6	9 16	9 16		9 20	10 6	10 44	...		11 6	12 6	12 46	1 1				1 6	2 26	2 26
e	,,	5 3	5 47	6 43	8 8	9 18	9 18		9 38	10 8	10 46	...		11 8	12 8	12 48	1 3				1 8	2 28	2 28
slade	,,	5 5	5 49	6 45	8 10	9 20	9 20	August and September only.		10 20	10 48	...	August and September only.	11 20	12 20	12 50	1 5	August and September only.			1 20	2 30	2 30
ersgate Halt	,,	5 7	5 51	6 47	8 12	9 22	9 22				10 50	...				12 52	1 6					2 32	2 32
chwick	,,	5 9	5 53	6 49	8 14	9 24	9 24				10 52	...				12 54	1 9					2 34	2 34
reham-by-Sea	,,	5 13	5 57	6 53	8 18	9 28	9 28				10 56	...				12 58	1 13					2 38	2 38
cing	,,	...	...	6 58		9 34	9 34				11 2	...					1 19					2 44	2 44
Bridge Halt	,,	...	...	7 1		9 37	9 37				11 5	...					1 22					2 47	2 47
thing	arr.	...	...	7 4		9 40	9 40				11 8	...				1 10	1 24					2 50	2 50
Worthing	dep.	...	...	...		9 41	10 0				B 11 45	...					1 25					2 51	2 51
ng	,,	...	...	...		9 43	10 3				B 11 48	...					1 28					2 53	2 54
mering	,,	...	...	...			10 7				11 52	...					1 32						2 58
inster Halt	,,	...	...	...			10 13				11 58	...					1 39						3 4
del	,,	...	...	...			10 19				12 4	...					1 44			2 32			3 10
ehampton	arr.	...	...	...			10 25					...					1 50			2 40			3 16
Junction		...	...	...							12 7												

B In July will run on to West Worthing, leaving Worthing at 11.9 and arriving at West Worthing at 11.11 a.m.

DOWN.   **WEEK DAYS.**

		p.m.		p.m.	p.m.	July p.m.	p.m.		p.m.	July p.m.	p.m.		p.m.	p.m.	p.m.	p.m.	p.m.	Not Sats. p.m.		
ghton	dep.	...		2 30	3 30	4 0	4 0		4 40	5 40	5 40		5 55	6 50	6 55	8 0	8 25	10 0	...	...
nd Road Halt	,,	...		2 33	3 33	4 3	4 3		4 43	5 43	5 43		5 58	6 53	6 58	8 3	8 28		...	...
e	,,	...		2 36	3 36	4 6	4 6		4 46	5 46	5 46		6 1	6 56	7 1	8 6	8 31	10 4	...	...
e Junction Halt	,,	...	August and September only.	2 38	3 38	4 8	4 8	August and September only.	4 48	5 48	5 48	August and September only.	6 4	6 58	7 3	8 8	8 33		...	...
e	,,	...		2 50	3 50				5 0				6 15		7 15	8 20			...	...
slade	,,	...		...	...	4 10	4 10			5 50	5 50			7 0			8 35	10 7	...	...
ergate Halt	,,	...		...	...	4 12	4 12			5 52	5 52			7 2			8 37		...	...
chwick	,,	...		...	...	4 14	4 14			5 54	5 54			7 4			8 39	10 10	...	...
reham-by-Sea	,,	...		...	...	4 18	4 18			5 58	5 58			7 8			8 43	10 14	...	...
cing	,,	...		...	...	4 24	4 24			6 4	6 4			7 14			8 49	10 20	...	...
Bridge Halt	,,	...		...	...	4 27	4 27			6 7	6 7			7 17			8 52		...	...
thing	arr.	...		...	...	4 30	4 30			6 10	6 10			7 20			8 55	10 25	...	...
thing	dep.	...		...	...	4 31	4 50				6 30						8 56		...	...
t Worthing	,,	...		...	...	4 33	4 53				6 33						8 58		...	...
ng	,,	...		...	...		4 57				6 37								...	...
mering	,,	...		...	...		5 3				6 43								...	...
inster Halt	,,	...		...	...		5 9				6 49								...	...
del	,,	4 0		...	...		5 15				6 55								...	...
ehampton	arr.	4 8		...	...		5 15												...	...
Junction																				

DOWN.   **SUNDAYS.**

		a.m.	a.m.	a.m.	a.m.	a.m.	a.m.	p.m.	p.m.	p.m.	p.m.	p.m.	p.m.	p.m.	p.m.	p.m.	p.m.	p.m.	p.m.	1 2 3 p.m.		
ghton	dep.	8 10	9 20	10 0	10 50	11 0	11 55	1 15	1 30	2 40	2 45	3 35	4 10	4 30	5 35	5 50	6 25	7 15	7 20	8 30	...	...
nd Road Halt	,,	8 13	9 23	10 3	10 53	11 58	1 18	1 33	2 43	2 48	3 38	4 13	4 33	5 38	5 53	6 28	7 18	7 23	...	...	...
e Junction Halt	,,	8 16	9 26	10 6	10 56	11 6	12 1	1 21	1 36	2 46	2 51	3 41	4 16	4 36	5 41	5 56	6 31	7 21	7 26	8 34	...	...
e	,,	8 18	9 28	10 8	10 58	11 8	12 3	1 23	1 38	2 48	2 53	3 43	4 18	4 38	5 43	5 58	6 33	7 23	7 28	...	...	...
e	,,			10 20		11 20	12 15		1 40	3 0		3 55		4 50	5 55		6 45		7 40	8 50	...	...
slade	,,	8 20	9 30		11 0			1 25		2 55		4 20		6 0			7 25		...	...
er-gate Halt	,,	8 22	9 32		11 2			1 27		2 57		4 22		6 2			7 27		...	...
chwick	,,	8 24	9 34		11 4			1 29		2 59		4 24		6 4			7 29		...	...
reham-by-Sea	,,	8 28	9 38		11 8			1 33		3 3		4 28		6 8			7 33		Not in September.	...
cing	,,	8 34	9 44		11 14			1 39		3 9		4 34		6 14			7 39		...	...
Bridge Halt	,,	8 37	9 47		11 17			1 42		3 12		4 37		6 17			7 42		...	...
thing	,,	8 40	9 51		11 21			1 46		3 16		4 41		6 21			7 46		...	...
st Worthing	arr.	...	9 53		11 23			1 48		3 18		4 43		6 23			7 48		...	...

Rail motor was the term used to describe the type of train shown in the second photograph in this album. It was developed partly to combat the competition from the electric tramway between Brighton and Shoreham. To confuse the passenger, normal trains were not shown in this 1910 Timetable.

WORTHING

1. Our journey commences at the west end of Worthing station where we see class H1 no. 38 – later named 'Portland Bill' by the Southern Railway – waiting to depart for Portsmouth. Notice the well dressed driver, with oilcan in hand, and the vaulted platform canopy of the town's second station, part of which was incorporated into the third station. The full story of the changes that have occurred here is told in the *Brighton to Worthing* album, in this series. (Author's Collection)

London Brighton & South Coast Railway.

Worthing to

Rowfant

1853 timetable

WORTHING.

	UP TRAINS.—DAILY.											SUNDAYS.				
WORTHING	7 36	8 10	9 30	10 13	12 55	3 5	5 20	6 15	7 5'	...	10 0	7 48	2 0	5 27	6 15	8 51
Brighton	9 0	8 45	10 0	11 0	1 45	4 0	6 0	6 50	8 35	...	10 30	8 20	2 30	6 15	6 45	9 30
London	11 30	10 5	11 30	1 0	3 45	5 45	—	9 5	10 30	...	—	10 30	4 40	9 0	—	—

	DOWN TRAINS.														
WORTHING	7 40	9 0	9 30	12 4	1 45	2 30	...	6 0	6 35	7 45	...	10 5	2 22	8 45
Chichester	—	9 50	—	12 40	—	3 7	...	6 42	—	8 30	...	10 55	3 2	9 35
Portsmouth		10 35		1 20		3 55	...	7 15		9 15	...	11 40	3 50	10 20

2. Class DI no. B228 with push-pull units stands in the up platform in 1930 en route to Brighton. Only the fireman travelled on the locomotive, the driver operating the controls by a servo-mechanism from a special compartment at the outer ends of the two pairs of coaches. The roof of the former corn exchange can be seen in the distance. (J.A.G. Coltas)

SOUTHERN RAILWAY.

This Ticket is issued subject to the By-laws Regulations & Conditions stated in the Company's Time Tables Bills & Notices Available on DAY of issue ONLY

5009   ANGMERING to   5009

Angmering   Angmering
Worthing   Worthing

WORTHING

THIRD CLASS   THIRD CLASS
Fare 7½d   Fare 7½d

NOTICE!

ON AND AFTER
MONDAY, JUNE 3rd,

LEE'S OMNIBUS

WILL LEAVE THE
White Horse Inn, Storrington,

EVERY

MONDAY, THURSDAY, AND SATURDAY,
At 8h. 45m., a. m.

Arriving at Worthing in time for the 10h. 42m. Train for Brighton; returning on the arrival of the 5h. 20m. Train from Brighton,

Until further Notice.

MAY 15th, 1861.

Horses and Flys may be had on application to Mr. LEE, White Horse Inn, Storrington.

Willins & Fatching, Printers.

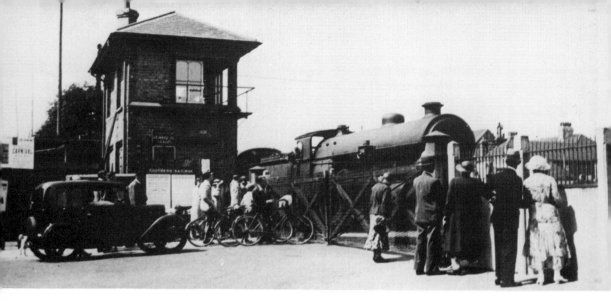

3. South Farm Road crossing was, and still is, the first of a large number of level crossings on the journey to Chichester. The signal box was known as West Box and later as 'B' box. It is now the only one at this station and since February 1961 has controlled lifting barriers, the first on the Southern Region, although the Festiniog Railway had attempted to install them at Penrhyndeudraeth some years earlier. The crossing was widened in 1934, but no footbridge or wicket gates were provided for pedestrians. (Madgwick Collection)

4. Looking east from 'B' box along Cross Street towards Central Station (as it was known between 1936 and 1968) with the locomotive water tower visible at the end of the street. On the left is a small goods yard (the nearest wagon is a horse box), the main yard and goods shed being beyond the station. Locomotive no. 336 is one of the ex LSWR T9 class (known as Greyhounds because of their speed), an example of which is operating on the Mid-Hants Railway, on loan from the National Railway Museum. (H.M. Madgwick/Lens of Sutton)

5. An 8-coach Portsmouth Harbour to Brighton stopping train enters Worthing in January 1982, in weather that forces most photographers to hibernate. Notice the Star of David in the cast stanchion brackets and the small position light signal on the end of the up platform which replaced its mechanical predecessor when 'A' Box was closed. (J.A.M. Vaughan)

WEST WORTHING

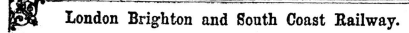

London Brighton and South Coast Railway.

WEST COAST LINE.

On and from Monday, November 4th, 1889,

A NEW STATION
AT
WEST WORTHING

(BETWEEN WORTHING AND GORING)
WILL BE OPENED FOR
PASSENGER TRAFFIC

And Trains running between Brighton, Barnham Junction and Portsmouth
will call at West Worthing as shown below :—

DOWN.						1st Class B				1 & 2 Class C	1 & 2 Class C	1st Class C D			SUNDAYS.		
	A.M.	A.M.	A.M.	A.M.	A.M.	A.M.	A.M.	P.M.	P.M.	P.M.	P.M.	P.M.	P.M.	P.M.	A.M.	P.M.	P.M.
Victoria (West End) .... dep.	..	..	7 35	..	10 0	11 10	..	1 50	..	4 30	..	..	5 55	..	7 0	1 10	5 50
Kensington (Addison Road) ,,	..	..	7 7	..	9 33	11 15	..	..	..	..	..	..	5 10	..	..	1 2	5 42
London Bridge (City) .. ,,	..	..	6 30	7 50	9 30	..	11 0	..	2 0	..	5 0	6	..	..	7 0	1 20	6 0
Brighton .... ,,	6 30	7 35	8 50	10 15	11 35	11 15	1 15	3 50	3 50	6 0	6 0	6 25	6 25	8 45	..	9 30	8 15	8 50
WEST WORTHING .. arr.	7 6	8 7	9 21	10 43	12 5	12 5	1 52	4 23	4 25	3 25	7 0	7 0	9 22	..	10 5	3 49	9 25

UP.	1st Cl. C	1st Class		1 & 2 Class C	1 & 2 Class C					1st Class B		C			SUNDAYS.		
	A.M.	A.M.	A.M.	A.M.	A.M.	A.M.	A.M.	P.M.	P.M.	P.M.	P.M.	P.M.	P.M.	P.M.	A.M.	P.M.	P.M.
WEST WORTHING .. dep.	6 43	8	8 8	8	8 24	9 49	9	10 51	12 58	2 49	4 50	4 50	7 43	7 43	8 15	5 46	8 10
Brighton .... arr.	7 20	8 38	8 38	8	8 28	9 49	9	10 51	1 30	3 15	5 30	5 30	8 15	8 15	8 50	10 24	8 15	5 46	8 10
London Bridge (City).... ,,	9 0	9 55	..	10 43	11	11 15	12 27	1 17	3 27	6 43	..	8 33	Sats. 10 33	..	12 15	10 43	8 15	11 20
Kensington (Addison Road) ,,	9 26	..	..	11 3	..	11 33	12 55	2 6	4	3 5	6 53	7 30	8 28	only. 10 51	..	11 43	8 23	..
Victoria (West End) .... ,,	9 11	..	10 5	10 54	..	11 25	12 32	1 44	3 32	5	4	6 55	4	55	10 40	..	10 56	8 16	11 29

B The Pullman Limited Trains between Victoria and Brighton,
London and Brighton. C Pullman Cars are run in these Trains between
D On Saturdays only this Train will be 1st and 2nd Class.

DOWN.	WEEK DAYS.										SUNDAYS.		
	A.M.	A.M.	A.M.	A.M.	P.M.	P.M.	P.M.	P.M.	P.M.	P.M.	A.M.	P.M.	P.M.
WEST WORTHING .. dep.	7 5	8	9 21	10 43	12 5	1 52	4 23	6 25	7 0	9 22	10 5	3 49	9 25	..
Littlehampton .... arr.	8 15	8 38	10 18	11 25	12 47	2 20	4 50	6 55	7 40	9 56	11 10	4 15	10 15	..
Bognor .... ,,	8 10	8 36	10 2	11 28	12 55	2 48	5 6	7 12	7 40	10 3	11 58	4 53	10 5	..
Chichester.............. ,,	..	8 47	10 2	11 28	12 45	2 35	5 6	7 2	7 42	10 4	10 44	4 28	10 6	..
Portsmouth Town ...... ,,	..	9 25	10 40	12 2	1 21	3 15	5 44	7 33	8 20	10 40	11 20	5 0	10 45	..
Portsmouth Harbour .. ,,	..	9 30	10 45	12 7	1 27	3 20	5 49	7 38	..	..	11 49	5 15	..	..

UP.	WEEK DAYS.										SUNDAYS.		
	A.M.	A.M.	A.M.	A.M.	A.M.	P.M.	P.M.	P.M.	P.M.	P.M.	A.M.	P.M.	P.M.
Portsmouth Harbour .. dep.	..	..	8 10	8 45	11 30	1 20	2 20	6 15	..	7 10	..	..	5 50	..
Portsmouth Town ...... ,,	..	..	8 15	9 0	11 35	1 25	3 25	6 20	..	6 50	..	6 15	3 59	7 20	..
Chichester .... ,,	..	..	8 43	9 34	12 14	2 6	4 3	7 1	..	9 25	..	6 51	4 24	7 55	..
Bognor .... ,,	..	7 30	8 42	9 37	12 5	1 55	4 8	6 42	7 17	9 25	..	6 50	4 5	8 0	..
Littlehampton .... ,,	6 15	..	9 0	9 20	12 28	2 0	4 22	7 5	..	9 20	..	6 45	4 40	7 50	..
WEST WORTHING .. arr.	6 43	8	8	9 24	10 15	12 58	2 48	4 50	7 43	9	9 57	7 32	5	8 38	..

ALL TRAINS are 1st, 2nd & 3rd CLASS except where otherwise stated.

POSTAL TELEGRAPHS.— By appointment of the Postmaster-General, West Worthing will be a Postal Telegraph
Station for the receipt and despatch of Telegrams to and from all parts.

☞ *For further particulars of Train Service, see Sheet Time Tables, Nos. 1 and 3.*

6. An early postcard view of West Worthing station, which was opened in 1889 as the urban area of Worthing expanded. A goods yard was added in the summer of 1905 in response to pressure from local horticulturalists. (M.J. Joly Collection)

London Brighton & South Coast Railway.

West Worthing to
Basingstoke
L. & S. W. R.

7. Soon after electrification of the London to West Worthing route in 1933, we see the same locomotive as shown in picture no. 4 (but with its chimney carrying a capuchon, which was later removed). On the up line stands one of the former London suburban electric sets, which were used on the stopping trains to Brighton for a year or two until the new 2 BIL and 2 HAL sets were ready. (H.M. Madgwick/Lens of Sutton)

8. Tarring Road crossing (just east of West Worthing station); West Worthing box and B4 class no. 2042, in the 1930s, soon after the introduction of the Belisha beacon. Anyone for tennis? (Madgwick Collection)

1898

Allotment Gardens

West Worthing
Station

S.P.

S.P.

3 ft. R.H.

CANTERBURY ROAD

ST DUNSTAN'S ROAD

A

Dov

9. Following this incident in November 1969, the awning was removed and during the next year total demolition of the station was announced. This has not happened yet, although the platform canopies have been lost. (J.A.M. Vaughan)

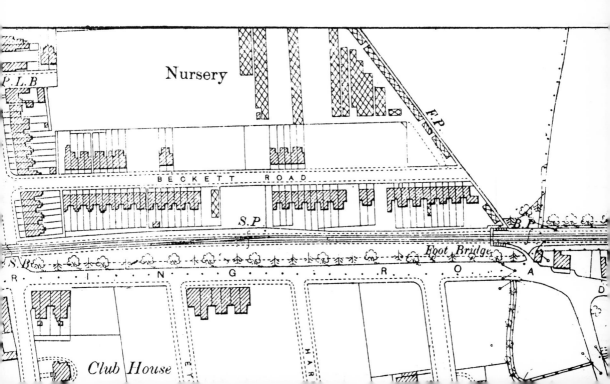

10. Two 2 BIL units have just arrived with a Brighton to West Worthing stopping train. The driver removes the headcode stencil whilst the guard places the tail lamp on what will be the rear of the train for the return journey. The train would then run into the siding to the west of the station, between the up and down lines, finally reversing into the up platform. (J.A.M. Vaughan)

1912

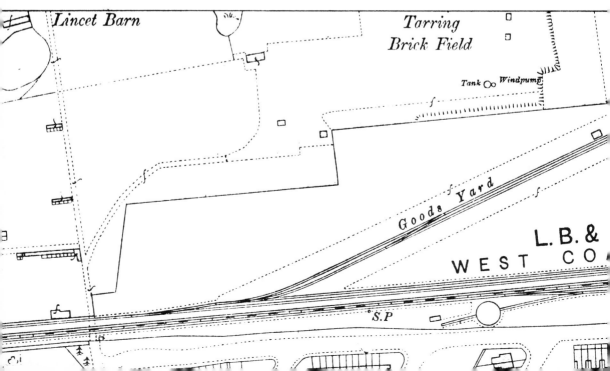

11. Unit 6046 leads with the 15.52 Brighton to Littlehampton train about to enter West Worthing station on 14th April 1982. Lifting barriers replaced the gates in December 1967 and six years later their control was linked to the traffic lights at the adjacent road junction, thus facilitating road traffic flow. (J. Scrace)

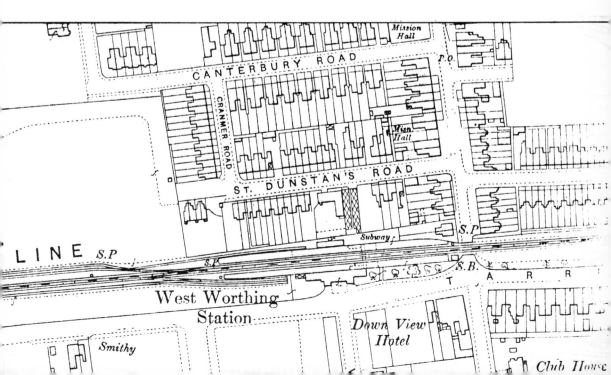

12. The carriage sheds during construction in 1932. The shed contains 3 roads, each capable of holding 12 cars. On the left is the locomotive siding (note the ashes) at the end of which is the water tower and turntable. The Brighton-bound locomotive is an ex-LSWR 4-4-0, class L12. (Lens of Sutton)

1932

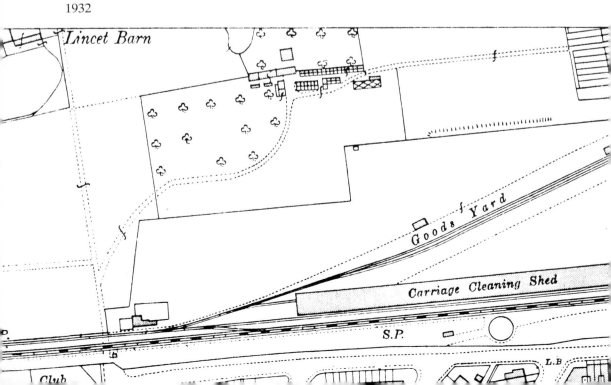

13. A Portsmouth-bound train heads west past the allotments and the newly completed carriage sheds, prior to completion of electrification to that city in 1938. (Lens of Sutton)

SOUTHERN RAILWAY.
CHEAP DAY TICKET
Available as advertised.
West Worthing to
SOUTHAMPTON DOCKS AND BACK
THIRD CLASS
INCLUDING CRUISE IN
SOUTHAMPTON WATER
FOR CONDITIONS SEE BACK.

0083 0083

14. Having run non-stop through the station, this fast train to Portsmouth Harbour is about to pass under Elm Grove footbridge on 14th April 1982, past the reversal siding. The sidings on the extreme left have been used occasionally in recent years for the unloading of stone trains. (J. Scrace)

15. Two coaches with an unusual career. Built for steam haulage on the LSWR, in SR days they were fitted with electric jumper cables and ran between two 3-car electric sets at peak periods. They are seen in the goods yard in June 1950, in semi-retirement, being used as temporary offices (D. Cullum)

London Brighton & South Coast Railway.

West Worthing to

Earlswood

0651
SOUTHERN RAILWAY.
HOLIDAY TICKET
Available as advertised.
to WEST WORTHING
Via
Third Class
FOR CONDITIONS
SEE BACK
SOUTHERN RAILWAY.
HOLIDAY TICKET
Available as advertised.
West Worthing to
Via
Third Class
0651

16. Elm Grove crossing in 1970 with Mr Bert Stagg officiating. Attendance was withdrawn on 26th June 1971, when the previously mentioned footbridge was brought into use. (J.A.M. Vaughan)

DURRINGTON

17. Ex-LSWR class S11 no. 395 passes under the new road bridge with the 11 a.m. Portsmouth to Brighton train on a misty November day in 1935. The site engineer was Henry Greenly, better known for his earlier work designing miniature locomotives, particularly those on the Romney, Hythe & Dymchurch Railway. (Madgwick Collection)

18. Soon after the opening of the station on 4th July 1937, we see a former LBSCR class E4 tank rumbling through with an eastbound freight train. (C. Fry Collection)

19. The modern 'Southern' style station, with extensive use of concrete, seen soon after the completion of electrification. It should be compared with the next photograph, which clearly shows the development of the area. (Lens of Sutton)

20. Photographed in 1967, we see 4-BIG unit no. 7047 with a Littlehampton to Victoria train. The Inland Revenue offices are on the left of the picture and Highdown Hill is on the extreme right. Durrington has never been provided with goods facilities. (J.A.M. Vaughan)

GORING

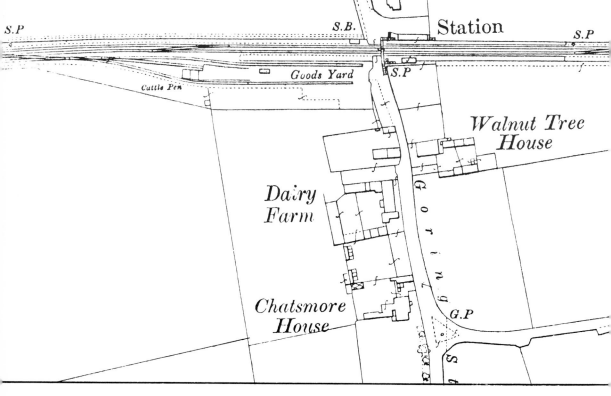

S.P S.B. Station S.P

Goods Yard S.P

Cattle Pen

Walnut Tree House

Dairy Farm

Goring

Chatsmore House

G.P

The track plan as shown on this 1932 map was almost unaltered throughout the life of the goods yard, until its closure in 1962. GP stands for guide post, which was at the point where Goring Way now runs westwards. (J.A.M. Vaughan)

21. Probably the least changed station on the line. This early postcard view shows a change of shade in the roof indicative of a possible earlier extension of the building. The abolition of oil lamps and the change of name to Goring-by-Sea took place in 1908. Later changes included the provision of a small platform canopy on the up side. (Lens of Sutton)

22. Looking south along Goring Street towards the level crossing. The LBSCR style gates remain in use to this day. On the right is the back of the signal box. Work commenced in the 1930s on a road bridge to the east of the station and the approach embankments still exist today. It seems that the Southern Railway demanded provision for quadruple track but the local authority refused. (Lens of Sutton)

1853 departures.

GORING.

GORING to	DAILY.				SUNDAYS.		
GORING to Brighton or London	7 28	10 6	2 55	7 40	7 41	5 18	8 48
GORING to Portsmouth	9 5	9 35	1 50	7 50	10 10	8 50	

Some of these trains go to Arundel only.

23. Class T9 loco no. 704 with a troop train on the wrong road on 11th August 1938. Perhaps it was being propelled along the down line prior to stabling in the goods yard or maybe there was engineering work on the up line. (Lens of Sutton)

24. Soldiers of the London Scottish Regiment entraining at Goring-by-Sea. Large numbers of soldiers often camped on the side of High-down Hill during summer months. Nearby fields had served as an airfield during World War I. (Madgwick Collection)

SOUTHERN RAILWAY

(7/47) 6M

TO

Stock 787

GORING-BY-SEA

25. An eastbound freight labours past the diminutive goods shed, hauled by class N no. 31835, accompanied by a smoke screen which is about to change the complexion of the photographer on the footbridge. (E. Gamblin)

26. From September 1961, one of the Brighton to West Worthing stopping trains was extended to Goring each morning for the benefit of school children and is seen here on the crossover near the goods yard in mid-winter. (J.A.M. Vaughan)

27. Ferring level crossing – November 1977. Note the original knapped flint and brick crossing keeper's cottage and cast-iron lattice windows. This was one of the first crossings to have an anti-skid surface of bauxite and resin on its timber decking. Plans for a station at this well populated location have not so far matured due to lack of the necessary financial contribution towards its cost from the local authorities. (C. Durrant)

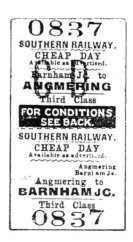

28. The original crossing cottage at Roundstone, with ground frame and attendants hut. It is the next public road crossing after Ferring. (Lens of Sutton)

29. Roundstone level crossing after the construction of the 'lean-to' type cabin. This structure is slightly unusual in as much as it is raised on a brick pier to give the crossing keeper a better view of traffic at this rather hazardous road junction. The gates are "Southern" pattern – timber and wire mesh construction – which can be compared with the LBSCR pattern in the previous photograph. (P. Hay)

ANGMERING

30. The original station was replaced in the 1860s and is shown here after a repaint around 1908. The signal box at the end of the platform dates from 1877. A crossover between platforms is unusual, but since it was probably not used in connection with passenger trains, its proximity to the signal box would have conveniently reduced point rodding. (Lens of Sutton)

1853 train service.

A N G M E R I N G.								
DAILY.						SUNDAYS.		
ANGMERING to Brighton or London ... 7 21	10 0	2 50	6 0	7 35		7 35	5 12	8 42
ANGMERING to Portsmouth 9 11	9 40	1 55	7 56			10 15	8 55	
The 9.40 and 1.55 trains stop at Arundel.								

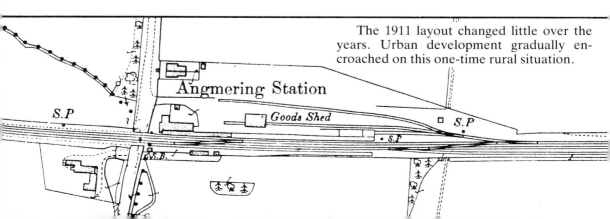

The 1911 layout changed little over the years. Urban development gradually encroached on this one-time rural situation.

S.P

Angmering Station

S.P

Goods Shed

S.P

S.P

S.B.

31. Ex-LBSCR class H2 no. 2422 enters Angmering on 22nd August 1936 with a Bognor to Victoria train. This was one of a class of six "Atlantics" designed by D.E. Marsh and built at Brighton in 1911-12. This particular engine was the first to be painted malachite green (in 1946) but was repainted in lined-black in 1951 and condemned in 1956. (H.C. Casserley)

32. Ex-LBSCR class H2 *Trevose Head* leaving Angmering with the Hoover Express (was it vacuum fitted?) on 29th October 1938, the year in which steam-hauled passenger trains had become a rarity on this section of line. (Lens of Sutton)

33. The concrete footbridge erected by the Southern Railway carries a banner repeater signal, as the bridge restricts visibility of the down starting signal. The shelter to the right of the goods shed was used for loading horticultural traffic. For many years a van train departed from Chichester at 11.35, picking up at Barnham and Angmering and conveying tomatoes, flowers, etc., to Bricklayers Arms in south-east London, where there were connecting services to the markets of the Midlands. Notice how much the platform has been extended. (P. Hay)

1853 train service with road connections.

ARUNDEL AND LITTLEHAMPTON.

	UP TRAINS.—DAILY.												SUNDAYS.					
ARUNDEL	7 14	8 0	9 20	9 55	12 40	2 45	3 15	...		5 55	7 30	...	7 25	...	5 4	...	8 36
Brighton	9 0	8 45	10 0	11 0	1 45	3 40	4 0	...		7 0	8 35	...	8 30	...	6 30	...	9 30
London	11 30	10 8	11 30	1 0	3 45	5 45	5 45	...		9 5	10 30	...	10 30	...	9 0	...	—

	DOWN TRAINS.—DAILY-																
ARUNDEL	9 20	...	...	...	12 18	2 45	...		6 15	8 6	10 25	...	2 36	9 5
Chichester.........	9 50	...	...	...	12 40	3 7	...		6 42	8 30	10 55	...	3 2	9 30
Portsmouth	10 35	...	...	...	1 20	3 55	...		7 15	9 15	11 40	...	3 50	10 20

	DAILY.						SUNDAYS.				
GARWOOD'S OMNIBUS leaves the Norfolk Arms, Arundel, for the Station as follows during the month......	6.45	8.50	11.50	2.15	5.25	7.0	6 55	9 55	2 5	4 35	8 5

	DAILY.						SUNDAYS.				
SPARKS'S OMNIBUS leaves the Norfolk Hotel, Littlehampton, for the Station, at the annexed times	6 54 9 0	9 30 11 56	1 45 2 25	2 55 5 35	6 30 7 10		7 3 	10 5 	2 17 	4 44 	8 16

LYMINSTER

34. A postcard view of Lyminster crossing c 1910. This signal box dates from 1877 but the crossing keeper's cottage is the original 1845 structure. Lifting barriers were brought into use in November 1963 and the signal box taken out of use in 1980. (Lens of Sutton)

35. A new halt was opened at Lyminster for the rail-motor service in 1907, but it was closed in 1914. It was nearer to the level crossing than the previous station. If a future Dr. Beeching axed the Littlehampton branch, maybe yet another station would appear on this site. (M.J. Joly Collection)

36. The original Lyminster station which opened in March 1846 (known as Littlehampton and Arundel) was a terminus until June of that year, when the line to Chichester was opened. The station then became known simply as Littlehampton. In 1850 the name changed again, this time to Arundel and Littlehampton, the reverse of the original name. In 1863, upon the opening of the Littlehampton branch, the station closed. This view, taken in the 1930s, shows a spacious goods shed, which survives today and is thought to have been used as an engine shed until 1863. (Lens of Sutton)

37. Arundel Junction, as seen from the top of a signal post in September 1929 by a professional signal engineer/amateur photographer. Destinations of the tracks – bottom right, Littlehampton; bottom left, Ford; top left, Arundel and top right, Angmering. In the foreground is a warning board for a temporary speed restriction. (Late E. Wallis)

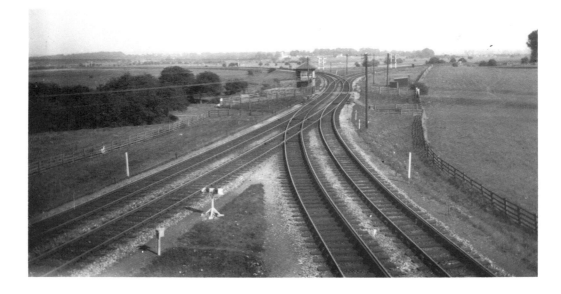

38. Arundel Junction box in April 1974, with an occupation crossing in the foreground. This signal box has since been demolished, the junction now being controlled from Arundel panel box. The signal box base was strengthened for use as an air-raid shelter. (J. Scrace)

39. The hourly service between Littlehampton and Victoria via Worthing was operated by 6-PUL units until 1965. These sets were unusual in having two motor bogies on both outer coaches and, more obviously, a distinctive chocolate and cream Pullman Car sandwiched between the other-wise uniform green coaches. The Little-hampton branch received colour light signals when electrified in 1938. One of them can be seen, under the semaphore, at the limit of that resignalling scheme. Photograph dated 5th March 1956. (E. Gamblin)

LITTLEHAMPTON

40. Looking north, around the turn of the century, there is ample evidence of the typical oil-lit four-wheeled coaches of the period and the then popular tarpaulin-covered goods wagons. (Lens of Sutton)

41. The symmetry of design apparent at Portslade, Steyning and West Worthing was also shown in the original terminal building, opened in 1863. The building on the left remains in use today, housing the area inspector and also gives permanent way staff accommodation. (Lens of Sutton)

42. Looking towards the buffer stops, we see a profusion of enamelled steel advertisement panels on the back wall of the station with an attractive scalloped platform canopy, part of which still stands today. On the extreme left is the locomotive shed, of which more will be seen later. (Lens of Sutton)

1879 six inch scale map.

1932 six inch scale map.

43. The original signal box, photographed in June 1886. (National Railway Museum)

0166
SOUTHERN RAILWAY.
Issued subject to the Bye-laws,
Regulations & Conditions in the
Company's Bills and Notices.
ANGLER
Available on Day of issue only
Littlehampton to
VICTORIA
Via Brighton or Horsham
Third Class
NOT TRANSFERABLE
SOUTHERN RAILWAY
ANGLER
Available on Day of issue only
Victoria to
LITTLEHAMPTON
Via Brighton or Horsham
Third Class
0166

44. E. Tanner, stationmaster for approximately 30 years, from 1892. (H.J.F. Thompson Collection)

45. This event on 4th August 1920 was much photographed, but we have chosen two views that we believe are previously unpublished.

In the background is the Locomotive Inn – nearly a very apt name under the circumstances. (H.J.F. Thompson Collection)

46. The brakes failed to function as the train entered the station at 30 m.p.h. carrying 30 passengers, 13 of whom were injured. This accident was the result of the air brake hose of the engine being wrongly connected to the first coach, which had other hoses for use with the push-pull controls. The failure of the guard to notice this error was also criticised at the inquiry. Note the gas cylinder wagon on the left. (Lens of Sutton)

47. One of Harris's horse buses outside the station during the late '20s in the care of 'Jumbo' Spicer, photographed before Harris's vehicles were taken out of service – defeated by Southdown Motor Services. The station was largely demolished in 1937, but lack of agreement with the local authority delayed reconstruction and the temporary structure remains in use today. (H.J.F. Thompson Collection)

SOUTHERN RAILWAY.
This Ticket is issued subject to the By-laws Regulations & Conditions stated in the Company's Time Tables Bills & Notices
Available on DAY of Issue ONLY
2592   **LITTLEHAMPTON**   2592
TO
ARUNDEL
3rd CLASS.   (S. 2)   3rd CLASS.
Fare 5½d.   Fare 5½d.

5603
L. B. & S. C. Ry.
This half available for 2 Days including Date of Issue and return.
See conditions at back
CHICHESTER TO
LITTLEHAMPTON
Third Cl. 1s. 9d.

LONDON BRIGHTON & SOUTH COAST RAILWAY.

HALF-DAY TRIP

TO
(LONDON BRIDGE STATION)

LONDON

Wednesday, Aug. 17th.

Leaving at	FROM	RETURN FARES. 3rd Class.
p.m.		
1 15	BOGNOR	
1 35	BARNHAM JUNC. .	**3/-**
1 30	LITTLEHAMPTON .	
1 45	ARUNDEL	

Returning same day from LONDON BRIDGE 12.5 midnight.

☛ ALLOWING OVER EIGHT HOURS IN LONDON.

CHILDREN UNDER TWELVE YEARS OF AGE, HALF-PRICE.

Passengers with Luggage will not be allowed to travel by this Train.

Tickets not transferable; only available to and from the Stations named thereon, by the Excursion Train, and on the date of issue. No allowance will be made for any Excursion Ticket lost, mislaid or not used.

WILLIAM FORBES, General Manager.

Waterlow & Sons Limited, Printers, Dunstable and London.

48. A trio of I3s off excursion trains grace the approach to the 2-road locomotive shed of 1863, part of which remains in use today as the parcels office by platform 4 and also houses railway staff and supervisors. The shed was a sub-shed of Bognor and closed in 1937. (Lens of Sutton)

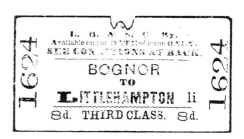

50. The staff cycle shed in 1951 gave employees a nostalgic reminder of earlier travelling conditions. Such psychotherapy might have been better applied to certain groups of complaining passengers. (British Rail)

49. BR class 4 no. 76008 on a Southampton train, passing the gasworks on 3rd August 1953, with two elderly LSWR compartment coaches at the head of the train, followed by a rake of Maunsell corridor coaches. Beyond the train is the two-storey goods shed. (S.C. Nash)

51. Outside the carriage sheds, built for the new electric trains in 1938, we see the shunter with his hand on a ground frame lever, awaiting the appropriate bell code from the signal box to be sounded in the open control box behind him. The class C2X no. 32522 was photographed here on 7th February 1956, about four years after it had been recovered from the bottom of a stream near Midhurst. That predicament is illustrated in our *Branch Lines to Midhurst*. (E. Gamblin)

52. The present signal box still controls the station area, although not with its original semaphore equipment, that having been replaced by colour lights in 1938. (J. Scrace)

53. An unusual train arrived on 11th November 1982 and stopped by the new carriage washing plant seen in the foreground. The Pullman coaches are those of the British part of the Venice-Simplon-Orient Express, which usually runs between London and Folkestone Harbour. On that day it had been chartered by Goodwood racegoers who had travelled in it as far as Arundel. The locomotive is class 73/1 no. 73122 and behind it is 4-CAP unit no. 3302 on a Coastway service. (J.A.M. Vaughan)

London Brighton & South Coast Railway.

Littlehampton to

Balham

LITTLEHAMPTON WHARF

The LBSCR obtained parliamentary powers to operate a steamboat service to Dieppe from Littlehampton, whilst another operator offered a regular link with the Channel Islands. The following year saw a 30-ton wooden steamship running to and from Ventnor, in the Isle of Wight. Eventually, the principal trade was with Honfleur on the north coast of France, a little to the West of Le Havre. Why Honfleur, which is so little known on our shores today? Its hinterland produced many perishable commodities, including eggs, butter, fruit and vegetables.

These could thus be exported direct to England, without trans-shipment at Le Havre. By the mid-1870s, the average annual tonnages imported through Littlehampton were 4200 tons of eggs and 4500 tons of butter, as well as vast amounts of poultry, wine and the like. In 1880 over 100 colliers entered the port and also 2000 tons of sugar were landed, all of which kept the railway wharves very busy, although the regular Honfleur service had been transferred to the company's expanded harbour at Newhaven in 1878.

54. A gleaming new marine boiler has just been lifted off the trolley, using the hand operated crane, but the vessel to receive it does not appear in the picture which was taken in about 1905.
(H.J.F. Thompson Collection)

London Brighton & South Coast Railway Co.

NOVEMBER, 1869. NOVEMBER, 1869.

LONDON & HONFLEUR

Via LITTLEHAMPTON,
BEING THE

SHORTEST ROUTE TO CAEN, TOURS, & THE WEST & SOUTH-WEST OF FRANCE.

The Screw Steamers "RENNES," "CAROLINE," & "IDA" are appointed to sail with Passengers and Merchandise as under (weather and unavoidable circumstances permitting), in connection with the London Brighton and South Coast Railway and the Western Railway of France.

HUDSON'S. HOUSEHOLD FURNITURE REMOVALS AND DEPOSITORIES. **HUDSON'S.**

HUDSON'S. DEPOSITORIES—LONDON, NORWOOD JUNCTION, AND BRIGHTON. **HUDSON'S.**

LITTLEHAMPTON TO HONFLEUR.				HONFLEUR TO LITTLEHAMPTON.			
DATES.			STEAMER LEAVES LITTLEHAMPTON.	DATES.			STEAMER LEAVES HONFLEUR.
Tuesday	...	2nd November	8.30 p.m.	Tuesday	...	2nd November	8. 0 p.m.
Wednesday	...	3rd ,,	9.30 ,,	Wednesday	...	3rd ,,	8.40 ,,
Thursday	...	4th ,,	9.40 ,,	Thursday	...	4th ,,	9.30 ,,
Friday	...	5th ,,	10.20 ,,	Friday	...	5th ,,	10. 0 ,,
Saturday	...	6th ,,	11.15 ,,	Saturday	...	6th ,,	11. 0 ,,
Monday	...	8th ,,	11.30 ,,	Monday	...	8th ,,	11.30 ,,
Tuesday	...	9th ,,	Midnight.	Tuesday	...	9th ,,	Midnight.
Wednesday	...	10th ,,	Midnight.	Wednesday	...	10th ,,	3. 0 p.m.
Thursday	...	11th ,,	3.30 p.m.	Thursday	...	11th ,,	3.30 ,,
Friday	...	12th ,,	5. 0 ,,	Friday	...	12th ,,	5.20 ,,
Saturday	...	13th ,,	6.15 ,,	Saturday	...	13th ,,	6. 0 ,,
Monday	...	15th ,,	7.40 ,,	Monday	...	15th ,,	7.30 ,,
Tuesday	...	16th ,,	9.20 ,,	Tuesday	...	16th ,,	8. 0 ,,
Wednesday	...	17th ,,	9.20 ,,	Wednesday	...	17th ,,	8.30 ,,
Thursday	...	18th ,,	9.30 ,,	Thursday	...	18th ,,	9. 0 ,,
Friday	...	19th ,,	9.45 ,,	Friday	...	19th ,,	9.30 ,,
Saturday	...	20th ,,	10. 0 ,,	Saturday	...	20th ,,	10. 0 ,,
Monday	...	22nd ,,	11. 0 ,,	Monday	...	22nd ,,	11. 0 ,,
Tuesday	...	23rd ,,	11.30 ,,	Tuesday	...	23rd ,,	11.30 ,,
Wednesday	...	24th ,,	Midnight.	Wednesday	...	24th ,,	Midnight.
Thursday	...	25th ,,	Midnight.	Thursday	...	25th ,,	Midnight.
Friday	...	26th ,,	3. 0 p.m.	Friday	...	26th ,,	Midnight.
Saturday	...	27th ,,	4. 0 ,,	Saturday	...	28th ,,	3. 0 a.m.
Monday	...	29th ,,	6. 0 ,,	Monday	...	29th ,,	6. 0 p.m.
Tuesday	...	30th ,,	7.15 ,,	Tuesday	...	30th ,,	7. 0 ,,

Tickets not delivered at Honfleur after 9.0 p.m

FARES:—

		LONDON AND HONFLEUR.				LITTLEHAMPTON AND HONFLEUR.		
	First Class.	Second Class.	Third Class (Deck & Rail)		First Cabin.	Second Cabin.	Deck.
Single	21s. 0d.	15s. 0d.	12s. 0d.	Single	15s. 0d.	12s. 0d.	10s. 0d.
Return	31s. 6d.	22s. 6d.	18s. 0d.	Return	22s. 6d.	18s. 0d.	12s. 0d.

Children under Three Years of Age ... ... Free.
,, Three Years, and under Twelve Years ... ... Half Fare.
,, Twelve Years, and above ... ... Full Fare.

Passengers, First and Second Class, from or to London, are allowed to break their voyage at Brighton or Littlehampton, the Single Tickets being available Four Days: Returns, One Month.

CATTLE CAN NOW BE IMPORTED AT LITTLEHAMPTON FOR THE INTERIOR.

	Horses, Ponies & Mules, under 12 hands.		Two-wheel.	CARRIAGES. Four-wheel.		Dogs.
LONDON AND HONFLEUR	60s.	45s.	40s.	60s.	7s. 6d.
LITTLEHAMPTON AND HONFLEUR	40s.	25s.	27s.	40s.	5s. 6d.

Steward's Fee, 1s. First; 6d. Second Cabin, for each Adult Passenger.

Passengers can be booked from Brighton, Portsmouth, Midhurst, Hastings, St. Leonards, Tunbridge Wells, Red Hill Junction, Croydon, Norwood Junction, Kensington, Clapham Junction, and 43, Regent Circus, London, at the same Fares as from London.
NOTE.—The Time occupied in Transit by the Railway between Honfleur and
LISIEUX is ... ... 1 h. 22 m. 2nd Class Fare, 3s. 0d. } CAEN is ... ... 3 h. 0 m. 2nd Class Fare, 4s. 6d.

Honfleur is in daily direct Communication with HAVRE by Steamers, 30 minutes' passage, First Class, 1s.; Second Class, 7½d.;
ALSO BY PASSENGER GOODS TRAINS WITH

Lisieux, Caen, Bayeux, St. Lo, Carentan, Cherbourg, Argentan, Falaise, Angers, Tours & Nantes.

All Goods should be directed as follows:—"To HONFLEUR, viâ LITTLEHAMPTON, per LONDON BRIGHTON AND SOUTH COAST RAILWAY," directed in full, and may be delivered at the Willow Walk Station, Bricklayers' Arms; at the Thames Junction Wharf, Deptford; or can be carted in by the Railway Company at very moderate rates.
Parcels and Light Goods only can be delivered at the London and Brighton Company's Receiving Offices :- 23, Cannon Street, E.C.; Bolt-in-Tun, 64, Fleet Street, E.C.; 69, Old Bailey, E.C.; George and Blue Boar, 285, High Holborn, W.C.; Golden Cross, Charing Cross; 452, Strand, W.C.; 32, Regent Circus, W.; New White Horse Cellar, 67, Piccadilly, W.; and 216, Oxford Street, W.

THERE ARE NO PIER DUES OR CLEARING CHARGES AT LITTLEHAMPTON.

For further particulars apply to
LONDON .... E. L. LETHBRIDGE, at the General Offices of the London & Brighton Railway Company, St. Thomas's Street, London Bridge, and Victoria Termini, and 43, Regent Circus, Piccadilly.

LITTLEHAMPTON	J. B. Cass, Railway Wharf.	NANTES	
BRIGHTON	W. Hudson, 71, Queen's Road, Terminus Gates.	ANGERS	J. P. Lucas.
HONFLEUR	Quai de la Quarantaine. } E. L. LETHBRIDGE, Manager.	ST. NAZAIRE	
HAVRE	31, Quai Casimir-Delavigne.	L'ORIENT	

←

55. "Stand there whilst I take your photograph dear." Another deceitful photographer, more interested in the nautical array than in his offspring, also fortuitously recorded the contemporary railway scene at the same time. Notice the steam crane and train of coal wagons in the distance. (H.J.F. Thompson Collection)

56. Towards the end of World War I, captured German guns were an unexpected import that the LBSCR was expected to transport. In the subsequent War, a remarkable export was 18,000 tons of ammunition, all of which was shipped between D-Day and the end of August 1944. (H.J.F. Thompson Collection)

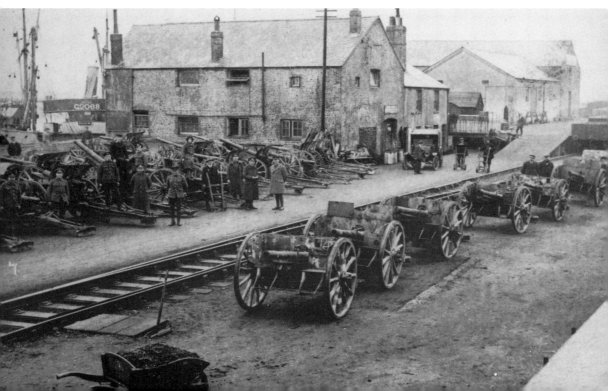

57. The *S.S. Pansy* in "dazzle" camouflage moored alongside the steam cranes. The harbour had been taken over completely by the military authorities in 1916. Note the ornate lamps on the warehouses. (H.J.F. Thompson Collection)

58. Terrier no. 32661 passes under one of the travelling dockside cranes in December 1955. The shunter seems to be protecting himself with a great-coat issued by Her Majesty rather than BR. (P. Hay)

ARUN BRIDGE

A Reprint from
" BRIGHTON, SHOREHAM AND CHICHESTER RAILWAY ILLUSTRATED " 1847

"THIS bridge. and the portion of the railway from Leominster to Chichester, was executed by Mr. Thomas Cox, Resident Engineer at Chichester ; Mr. Hale being the contractor, who employed Mr. Butt, of Littlehampton, to build this bridge, and to whom the workmanship does the greatest credit."

THE TELESCOPE BRIDGE OVER THE ARUN

THE ABOVE IS THE FIRST BRIDGE OF THE KIND EVER CONSTRUCTED

The first bridge was of an unusual telescopic type with a 34 ft. high frame running on 18 wheels, carrying a single railway track and subject to a 10 m.p.h. speed restriction. A further portion of track was mounted on wheels and this could be moved laterally to allow the main span to be withdrawn in it place.

59. The second Arun Bridge, completed in 1862, carried double track. The navigable channel width was reduced from 60 to 40 feet and is shown here, in a rare photograph of the bridge in the withdrawn position. (Lens of Sutton)

60. Locomotive no. 318 rumbles over the bridge with Ford station in the distance and the distinctive LBSCR headcode boards much in evidence. No. 318 was built in 1896 as class B2, converted to B2X in 1910 and withdrawn from service in 1930. (Lens of Sutton)

61. Class B4X no. 2067, in Southern Railway days, running onto the fixed span from the east. The bridge had been designed by Mr. Jacomb-Hood and built by Mr. Henry Grisell of the Regent's Canal Iron Works in London. The small cabin was provided for the comfort of the bridge gang. (Lens of Sutton)

62. Looking towards Ford with the bridge withdrawn for the passage of vessels. (WSCC Library Service)

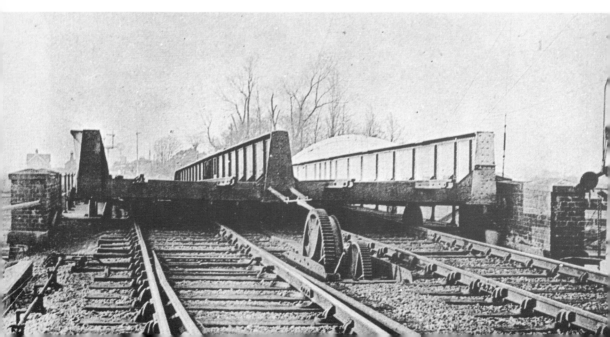

63. By the 1930s shipping had long ceased at Arundel and so it was decided to rebuild the bridge with a fixed span, in readiness for electrification. The scene depicts two 36-ton cranes working during the week-end of April 23-25, 1938. (H.J.F. Thompson Collection)

64. This is not a bridge testing exercise but merely three locomotives (nos. 31905, 45350 and 45187) running to Littlehampton to work return excursions, having been to Bognor M.P.D. for coaling during the day. (S.C. Nash)

FORD

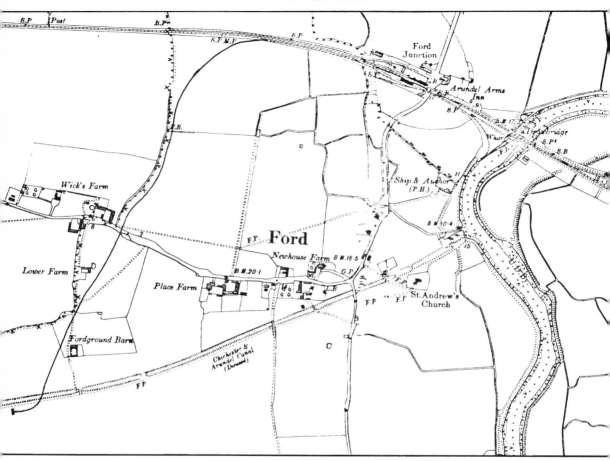

1912 map showing the branch to the wharf which was opened in May 1850. For many years a lime kiln was in use on this wharf. The approximate route of the branch built to serve the American military camp between 1916 and 1918 has been superimposed onto the 1912 six-inch scale map. SP indicates signal post and SB is the signal box at the west end of the station. The canal was the former Chichester & Arundel Canal, which at one time was part of an inland waterway between Portsmouth and London.

SOUTHERN RAILWAY.
(2/46) 12M   Stock
TO   787
FORD
(SUSSEX)

65. Stationmaster and staff at "Ford – for Littlehampton," the station's second name. When the coast line opened, this station was known as "Arundel". When the Southern Railway was formed in 1923, the name became "Ford (Sussex)", to avoid confusion with another station of the same name on that company's system in Devon. The suffix was dropped in 1964. (C. Fry Collection)

66. The elegant and popular Gladstone class locomotives were a familiar sight on the south coast in the early years of this century. No. 618 was actually called *Gladstone*, although it carried the number 214 until 1920. It is now preserved by the National Railway Museum at York. Note the water tower and wind-driven pump in the background of this photograph, taken in 1921. (O.J. Morris/Lens of Sutton)

67. Ford Shunting Box was at the west end of the station and controlled goods yard movements until 1930. Here we see class B2X no. 321 slowing to cross the bridge with an up train. (Lens of Sutton)

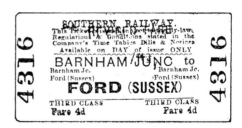

68. Looking east on 1st July 1923, showing the LBSCR style crossing gates and signal box. In the distance can be seen the junction signals, just over the river, and to their right the wharf branch dips steeply away. The small white building between the wharf and main lines was used at one period as a blacksmith's shop. (Late E. Wallis)

69. Class B2X no. B206 prepares to leave with a Portsmouth train in October 1932, the year before it was broken up, having run over a million miles in 36 years. The up goods is hauled by class C2X no. B553 and is passing the small goods yard which was closed in 1964. Note that the LBSCR type signals have been replaced. (H.C. Casserley)

70. The road from the station to the outskirts of Arundel was constructed and maintained by the railway company, who charged a toll for its use. The road was transferred to the West Sussex County Council on 31st December 1938. (Garland Collection)

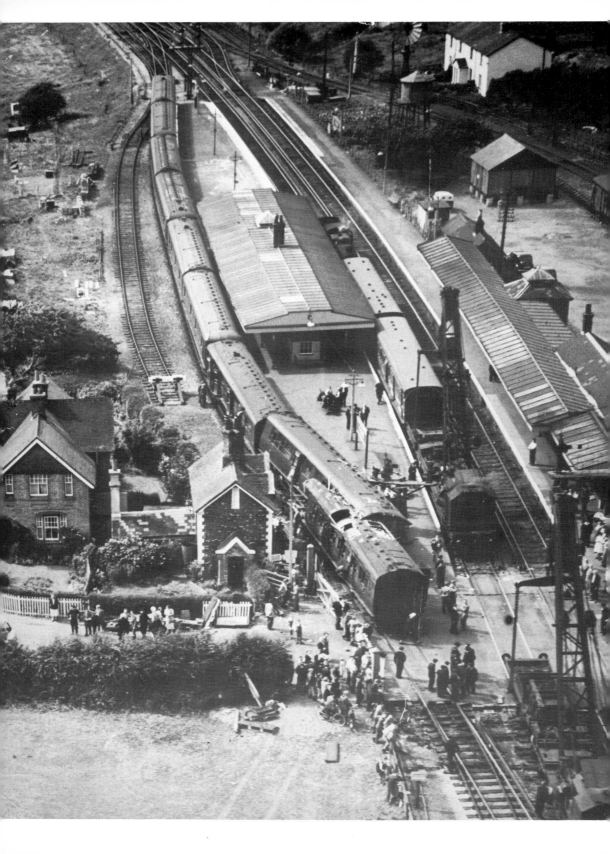

72. Co-Co electric locomotives were introduced in the early 1940s and were regularly used on Chichester-London freight runs. Owing to the risk of stalling when out of contact with the conductor rails on wide level crossings, flywheels were fitted to maintain momentum. Only three were built and were nicknamed *The Hornby's*. (E. Gamblin)

0198
SOUTHERN RLY.
This ticket is issued subject to th.
By-laws, Regulations and Condi
tions stated in the Company'
Time Tables, Bills and Notices.
Available for
includ'g d....e issue&ret'n

TO FORD [SUSSEX]
VIA
1st Cl. Fare
SOUTHERN RLY.
This half available for

FORD [SUSSEX]   to

VIA
1st Cl. Fare
0198

0250
SOUTHERN RAILWAY
Issued subject to the Bye-laws
Regulations & Conditions in the
Company's Bills and Notices.
DAILY WORKMAN
Littlehampton to
BRIGHTON
(Issued at Brighton)
Third Class. Fare 1/5
Available as advertised.
NOT TRANSFERABLE.

SOUTHERN RAILWAY
DAILY WORKMAN
Brighton to
FORD (SUSSEX)
Third Class. Fare 1/5
0250

71. On 5th August 1951, a 6-coach Brighton to Portsmouth train inexplicably ran past the inner home signal and collided at 18 m.p.h. with the rear of the 10.47 Three Bridges to Bognor, with which it was supposed to connect. The poor impact resistance of the wooden bodies is horrifyingly obvious. (D. Chown Collection)

73. The 2-BIL unit, the upper quadrant signals and the very lengthy crossing gates have all been scrapped since this picture was taken in July 1971. The latter were replaced by barriers in 1979. (J.A.M. Vaughan)

74. The 16.45 Littlehampton to Ford branch line train drifts into the loop, minus headcode, on 29th July 1971. Notice the guard's periscope on the roof, now another thing of the past. The unit is a 2-HAL. (J. Scrace)

YAPTON

75. Yapton crossing, scene of a fatal collision on 5th May 1967, was converted to lifting barriers two months later. The buildings are those of Yapton station, closed when Barnham was opened in 1864. Note the diversity of chimney pots and the milepost (21 from Brighton). (P. Hay)

1853 departure times.

YAPTON.

	DAILY.			SUNDAYS.		
YAPTON to Brighton or London		7 4	5 45	7 15	4 52	8 21
YAPTON to Portsmouth		9 30	8 16	10 34	9 14	

BARNHAM

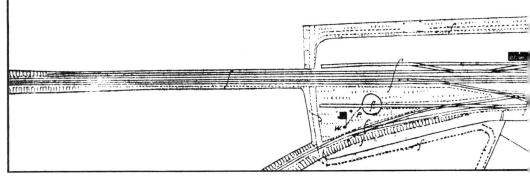

The 1876 map shows the lack of direct
branch line connection to the main line.

76. This is reputed to be the scene at the
opening of the Bognor branch on 1st June
1864. Behind the locomotive is a guards van,
followed by first, second and third class
coaches. The guard used his observatory to
check that the train had not lost any coaches
on its journey, a necessary precaution before
the advent of continuous brakes which are
applied automatically in the event of a
coupling failure.
(H.J.E. Thompson Collection)

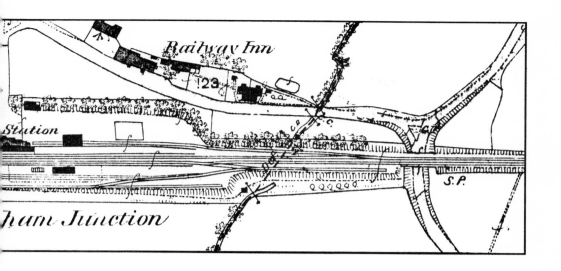

77. Another view of what was probably the first train to Bognor. Henfrey Smail described the locomotive as one of the early Sharps, of the series nos. 20-33, built between 1838 and 1849. (C. Fry Collection)

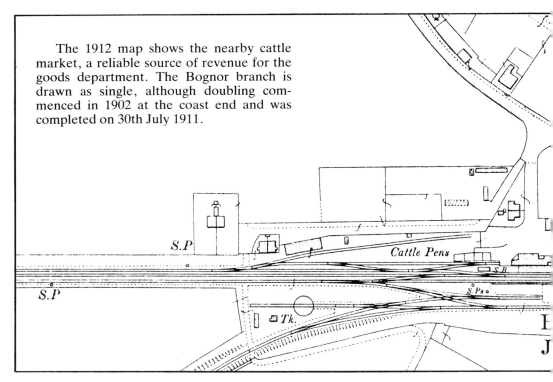

The 1912 map shows the nearby cattle market, a reliable source of revenue for the goods department. The Bognor branch is drawn as single, although doubling commenced in 1902 at the coast end and was completed on 30th July 1911.

78. Another Gladstone class to adorn our pages, this time no. 220 *Hampden*, withdrawn in 1911. Notice the slotted post branch signal with the spectacle-less semaphores (the lamp rotating on a separate bracket). This post has a more ornate finial than the main line signal of a later design. One of the ubiquitous Terriers is blowing off, on the branch train. At the time that this photograph was taken in 1901, there was no direct connection between the branch and the main line. (Lens of Sutton)

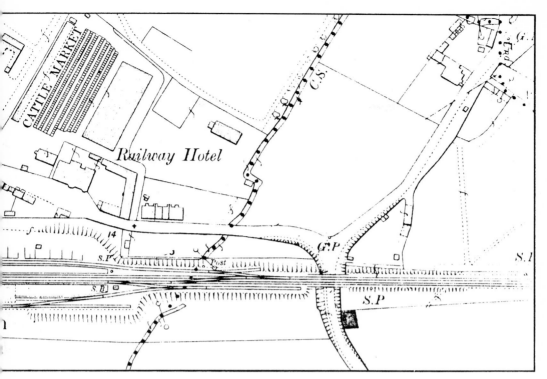

79. The station was extensively re-modelled with new signalling, signal box and down platform building with canopy, most of which remain today. The up platform facilities had not been altered when this photo was taken in 1930. Through trains to London from Bognor commenced in 1903, after the branch had been doubled and the junction rearranged. (O.J. Morris/Lens of Sutton)

80. Readers of our companion album *Brighton to Worthing* will have seen class I3 no. 2022 before, gracing the cover of that volume. Here she makes another attractive picture, whilst coming off the Bognor branch with an assortment of coaches, the first two being by Maunsell and the third is a Pullman. On the right is the shelter for horticultural traffic and a LBSCR milk van. (Lens of Sutton)

81. The white headcode disc indicates the front of the train. The driver can be seen at the end window, operating the locomotive by remote control, the fireman remaining alone on the footplate. We are looking towards Ford with the engine release roads on the right. These were eliminated at the time of electrification. (Lens of Sutton)

82. U1 class no. 31902 leaving Barnham with empty carriage stock for a return LMR excursion from Bognor Regis on 26th June 1953. The gantry on the left was used for heavy goods traffic. (S.C. Nash)

London Brighton and South Coast Railway.

Barnham Junction to

Amberley

83. Most fast trains from London divide at Barnham. Here we see the Portsmouth portion of the 14.28 ex-Victoria on 23rd September 1981, passing the impressive crossings on the Bognor branch. (J. Scrace)

BOGNOR

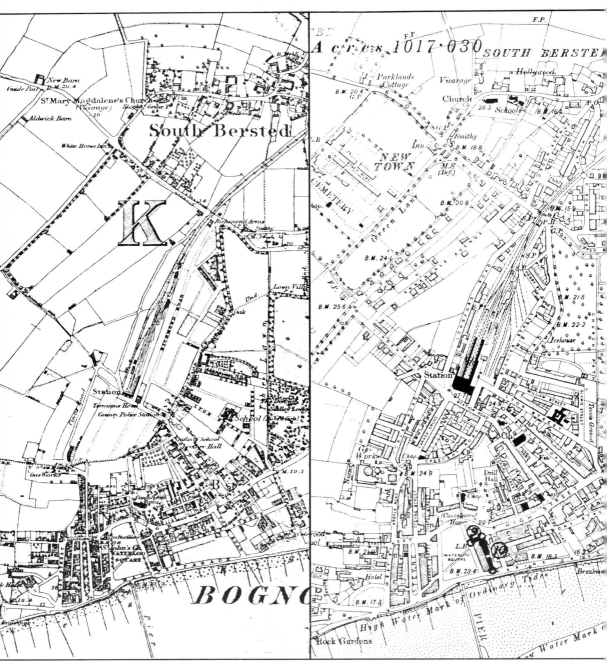

Six inch scale map of 1879 still showing the original single platform.

Six inch scale map of 1914 showing the revised layout.

84. The first station had only one platform and on 3rd March 1897 its canopy was destroyed during a storm. The goods shed (just visible on the left) and the main buildings were undamaged. (C. Fry Collection)

85. This unlucky station was next assaulted on 29th September 1899, when fire completely destroyed the buildings. Apparently, a coat had been left to dry on a stove! A temporary building was erected whilst a new station was designed and built. (West Sussex Library Service)

86. The imposing new station was completed in 1902 but suffered the same indignity as noble Kings Cross by having a string of small shops deposited in its shadow. (Lens of Sutton)

Part of the architects drawing for the reconstruction.

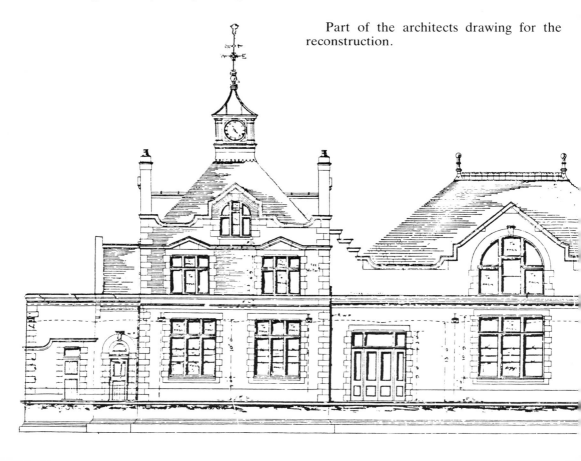

87. The smart station staff in May 1912 complimented the elegant station, with its fine vaulted roof over the concourse and glazed arches over the buffer stops. In the background is the unusual half-cupola of the refreshment room bay window, the latter remarkable for its curved glass. (National Railway Museum)

```
L. B. & S. C. & L. & S. W. RYS.
Available for 2 Days including Date of issue
BOGNOR     to      BATH
Via Havant, L. & S. W. Ry. & Templecombe
8s. 8d.  THIRD CLASS.  8s. 8d.
The connection of Trains not guaranteed
Not Transferable.      Issued subject to the
Conditions in the Time Tables of the respective
Cos' over whose Lines this Ticket is available.
        BATH          [SEE BACK
        SINGLE
```

1800 1800

L.B & S.C.RY
Bognor Station
D. KING

88. For many decades, free delivery of passengers' luggage was part of the railway company's service. D. King may have arrived but The King did not arrive until 1929, to give the town its suffix – Regis. During his period of residence, a special coach to convey state papers was added to certain London to Brighton trains and then run non-stop to Bognor. (L.C.G. Holden Collection)

89. Taken immediately after the re-opening in 1902, we see one of the D-tanks, no. 228 *Seaford* standing with a string of four-wheelers. The prevailing south-westerly wind is rapidly redirecting the surplus steam. (Lens of Sutton)

90. The new engine shed at Bognor, built in 1903, with part of the old shed on the left of the picture. The latter was demolished for the realignment of the new station and its approaches. The signal cabin was also constructed at this time, to replace the original box of 1876. The shed was a sub-shed of Horsham until 1926 and from 1941. It was closed in 1953 and demolished in 1956. (Lens of Sutton)

91. The 6-wheeled clerestory roofed coach in the foreground was one of only four such vehicles and was built in 1903. They consisted of a saloon compartment, a servants compartment and a luggage compartment, both saloon and servants compartments having their own toilet facilities. This particular vehicle started its life as no. 10. It was reclassified third (no. 301) in 1920 and withdrawn from service in 1925. By the time it was photographed at Bognor in February 1927 it had been relegated to shed foreman's office. The locomotive is class B4 no. B53, originally named *Sirdar* but renamed *Richmond* in 1906. (H.C. Casserley)

92. A quartet of D1s, specially posed for the photographer. When the Southern Railway took over the LBSCR locomotive stock in 1923, it gave a small prefix B to each number (to indicate Brighton origin) but from 1931 prefixed each number with a 2, thus B615, in the distance, still retained the earlier numbering system when this photograph was taken. (O.J. Morris/Lens of Sutton)

93. The new signal box, built on electrification in 1938, was adjacent to Bersted level crossing – the old Bersted Crossing Box, of original 1876 construction, had been on the opposite side of the crossing. This unique photograph of 30th June 1957 shows a LMR class 5 leaving Bognor Regis with a return excursion to Tring. This was the first time this class had visited the town. A road bridge has made the crossing redundant although the gates still remain in position. (E. Wilmshurst)

95. General view of the track layout in 1982, from the footbridge on the site of Bersted Crossing. The signal box in the foreground was opened in the year of electrification (1938) and contained 66 levers. It replaced two earlier boxes. At that time the platforms were lengthened and three berthing sidings, with concrete stages for use by carriage cleaners, were provided (seen on the right of the picture). (J. Scrace)

94. No. 73142 *Broadlands* with Pullman cars from the Venice-Simplon-Orient Express on 17th August 1982. Not for racegoers this time, but for filming purposes, necessitating the changing of the station nameboards to Folkestone Harbour! The engine release crossover at the far end of the platform is still controlled by nearby hand operated levers, in a Saxby and Farmer frame. (J. Scrace)

WOODGATE

96. Woodgate crossing was the site of the first Bognor station, in use until the branch opened. On the left, is the crossing keeper's cottage, probably dating from 1846. It has lost its lattice windows but retains an attractive wooden porch. The 1876 signal box is still in use as a block post, at least during the day, but will disappear when the £1m scheme to resignal the Barnham to Chichester line is implemented. The new lifting barriers are observed on closed circuit TV at Barnham signal box. (P. Hay)

The 1853 timetable, showing the connecting bus service.

BOGNOR.

	UP TRAINS.—DAILY.								SUNDAYS.				
BOGNOR	6 58	9 10	......	12 30	...	5 40	...		7 10	...	4 47	...	8 19
Brighton	9 0	10 0	......	1 45	...	7 0	...		8 30	...	6 30	...	
London	11 30	11 30	......	3 45	...	9 5	...		10 30	...	9 0	...	9 30
	DOWN TRAINS.—DAILY.												
BOGNOR	9 35	......	12 30	2 57	...	6 30	8 25		10 39	...	2 50	9 19	
Portsmouth	10 35	......	1 20	3 55	...	7 15	9 15		11 40	...	3 50	10 20	

SWAN'S OMNIBUS starts for the	DAILY.					SUNDAYS.				
Station at the following times............	6 0	8 20	11 30	2 0	5 0	6 35	9 30	2 0	3 45	7 30

DRAYTON

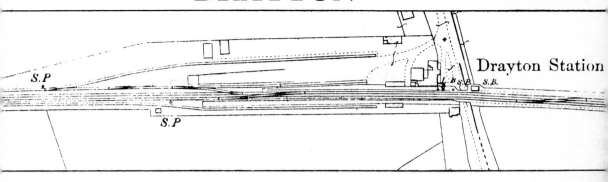

1912 map.

London Brighton & South Coast Railway.

Emsworth to

Drayton

97. This was one of the original stations on the line and was intended to serve the local agricultural community and the Goodwood racecourse, four miles to the north. Race traffic declined after 1881 when Singleton station was opened, as it was less than half that distance from the course.
(M.J. Joly Collection)

98. Another eastward view, this time from the top of the down starting signal post in May 1929, showing extensive goods facilities provided at this sparsely populated location. (Late E. Wallis)

99. Passenger services were withdrawn on 1st June 1930, but freight continued to be handled. The site became part of a WSCC highways depot but the gates and signal box have been retained, the latter being a block post controlling two crossovers. (Lens of Sutton)

SECOND SUPPLEMENT TO
NOTICE of SPECIAL TRAFFIC No. 31,

Week ending August 4th, 1877.

TO THE OFFICERS AND SERVANTS OF THIS AND OTHER COMPANIES CONCERNED.

Royal Special Train,

WITH

H.R.H. THE PRINCE OF WALES,

AND SUITE,

FROM DRAYTON TO VICTORIA.

(Via the Dorking and Mid-Sussex Direct Lines.)

☞ The exact departure of the Royal Train cannot be fixed, but the Train may be expected to leave Drayton about 5 p.m.

The starting time of the Royal Train from Drayton must be telegraphed to the various Stations and Junctions shown in the undermentioned Table.

The following Time Table shows the speed at which the Royal Train will be run from Drayton to Victoria, so that each Station Master will, on receipt of telegraphic advice that the Train has left Drayton, be able to fix the time due at the various Stations and Junctions shown, and regulate the working of the ordinary traffic accordingly.

On Friday, August 3rd.

UP.				arr.	pass.	dep.	UP.				arr.	pass.	dep.
					P.M.							**P.M.**	
DRAYTON ..	..	..	..		**0 00**		WARNHAM..	..	..	..	0 49		
Barnham Junction	..	..	..		0 7		Ockley..	..	..	..	0 55		
Ford Junction ..	..	..	..		0 11		Holmwood	..	..	..	1 0		
Arundel	..	..	..		0 14		Dorking	..	..	..	1 7		
Amberley	..	..	..		0 19		Leatherhead Junction	..	..	..	1 13		
Hardham Junction	..	..	..		0 24		Epsom Junction	..	..	..	1 18		
Pulborough	..	..	..		0 25		Sutton Junction	..	..	..	1 24		
Billingshurst	..	..	..		0 33		Mitcham Junction	..	..	..	1 29		
Stammerham Junction	..	..	..		0 40		Streatham Junction North	..	..	1 32		
HORSHAM ..	..	..			**0 45**		Balham Junction	..	..	..	1 36		
							Clapham Junction	..	..	..	1 40		
							York Road ..	..	..	..	1 43		
							VICTORIA ..	..	..	..	1 45		—

The Royal Special Train will leave Brighton, Empty, at 12.0 noon for Chichester, and return from Chichester to Drayton at once.

The Royal Special Train will leave Victoria, Empty, at 8.5 p.m. for Brighton, and run via Balham

100. A condition of the planning consent to dig gravel near Lavant, north of Chichester, was that the material must be transported by rail. A special block train of hoppers started running in January 1972 on part of the former Midhurst branch and terminating at Drayton. This traffic ceased in June 1981, but recommenced on 12th September 1983 with four trips per day on three days a week. Here we are looking west, with the cathedral spire in the distance. (V. Mitchell)

101. This and the previous photographs were taken on 8th January 1983, when the idle train was stored in the run-round loop. When loaded, it is normally propelled over the bridge on the left and the gravel is dis-charged into the water filled pit underneath. From this a drag-line excavator digs it out and in so doing carries out the primary wash-ing, removing large quantities of unwanted clay. (V. Mitchell)

102. Viewed from the bypass bridge on the same day, we see the 9.20 Brighton to Exeter train hauled by a class 33 diesel passing Portfield oil depot siding. This depot was built during World War II, presumably to supply the numerous RAF airfields on the coastal plain, and was reopened in 1978 as a distribution point for light heating oils. (V. Mitchell)

104. Looking west from the bypass bridge we see the extent of Bartholomews' sidings, which still carry a small traffic of imported grains used in the production of animal feed-stuffs, and, in the distance, Bognor Road bridge. (P. Hay)

103. Class I3 no. 2082 with a Brighton to Portsmouth train passing Bartholomew's sidings, between the wars. The level crossing was replaced by a single carriageway bridge for the Chichester bypass on 14th September 1944, eventually carrying dual carriageway. The signal box eventually gave way to a ground frame. (H. Gordon-Tidey)

105. Whyke Road crossing has remained unchanged for decades but the equipment shown in this 1974 photograph will disappear in the near future. Whyke was, for centuries a small country parish, only becoming merged with Chichester within the last 50 years. (E. Wilmshurst)

106. Basin Road crossing, only yards before Chichester station, was operated manually, not even by a wheel, until replaced by barriers in April 1973. Note the gas lamp between the crossing keeper's hut and the modern neon street light. The basin referred to was not for washing in – merely the city canal basin. (D. Cullen)

CHICHESTER

107. Looking west from Stockbridge Road crossing c 1880. The Chichester East Box in the foreground was opened in 1875 and replaced an earlier structure. The main station building was built by Robert Bushby in 1846/47 with the overall iron roof being supplied by Palmer, Green & Co, in the same year. The enclosing of the ends was authorised in 1860. (Late E. Wallis Collection)

1853 timetable.

CHICHESTER.

	UP TRAINS.—DAILY.										SUNDAYS.		
CHICHESTER-	6 45	9 0	...	......	12 20	2 55	5 30	...	...	7 0	4 36	8 8
Brighton	9 0	10 0	...	......	1 45	4 0	7 0	...	...	8 30	6 30	9 30
London	11 30	11 30	...	......	3 45	5 45	9 5	...	...	10 30	9 0	——
	DOWN TRAINS.												
CHICHESTER-	9 50	......	12 40	3 7	...	6 42	8 30	10 55	3 2	9 35
Portsmouth	10 35	......	1 20	3 55	...	7 15	9 15	11 40	3 50	10 20

108. Following removal of the overall roof a better impression can be gained of the elegant lines of this station. Chichester West Box, also opened in 1875, is visible beyond the end of the down platform. In 1906 the City Council was making vociferous complaints about the inadequate width of the platforms. The matter was remedied when the station was reconstructed in 1957-58. (Lens of Sutton)

110. Another rare photograph, an LBSCR road vehicle. Here we see no. 284 at the junction of New Park Road with St. Pancras, near the Eastgate of Chichester. (W. Dew Collections)

109. A rare photograph showing an ambulance train at Chichester during World War I. Injured soldiers were then taken by road to Graylingwell Military Hospital, north of the city. On the left is the bay platform for the branch line to Midhurst.
(W. Dew Collection)

111. No. B176 entering Chichester – change for Selsey on Sea – with a Portsmouth to Brighton train on 16th July 1927. This Gladstone class locomotive was scrapped two years later, aged 39. The branch line to Selsey is fully illustrated in our companion album of that title. (H.C. Casserley)

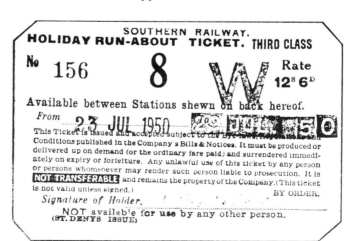

SOUTHERN RAILWAY.
HOLIDAY RUN-ABOUT TICKET. THIRD CLASS

No 156   8   W   Rate 12s 6D

Available between Stations shewn on back hereof.

From 23 JUL 1950

This Ticket is issued and accepted subject to the Bye-laws, Regulations and Conditions published in the Company's Bills & Notices. It must be produced or delivered up on demand (or the ordinary fare paid) and surrendered immediately on expiry or forfeiture. Any unlawful use of this ticket by any person or persons whomsoever may render such person liable to prosecution. It is NOT TRANSFERABLE and remains the property of the Company.(This ticket is not valid unless signed.)   BY ORDER.

Signature of Holder.

NOT available for use by any other person.
(ST. DENYS ISSUE)

112. The neglected state of the once opulent-looking up side building was evident when this photograph was taken, shortly before its demolition in 1957. The booking office window was more like the entrance to a small dog kennel and it was often necessary to rattle a few coins or produce an artificial cough to attract the attention of the hidden booking clerk. Alternatively, the sound of heavy boots on the suspended wooden floor of the booking hall could have the desired effect. (C. Attwell Collection)

SOUTHERN RAILWAY.
One Musical Instrument, Typewriter or other
article at Owner's risk (accompanied by Passenger)
ONE

Bognor Regis to

.... Rly.
Carriage Paid .... s. .... d.
This Ticket is available for one journey only
and must be given up at destination Station.

FOR CONDITIONS SEE BACK

0372   0372

113. Only a lone cyclist is delayed by the closure of Stockbridge Road gates by the signalman in the box tucked in beside the then covered footbridge. Class I3 no. 2027 accelerates towards Barnham, past the ivy clad police station, which housed army personnel during the last war and later was demolished to make way for the bus station. (Lens of Sutton)

SOUTHERN RAILWAY.
Available on the DATE of issue ONLY.
This ticket is issued subject to the Regulations
& Conditions stated in the Company's Time
Tables & Bills
CHICHESTER
TO
ANGMERING FOR EAST PRESTON
AND RUSTINGTON
THIRD CLASS.
1/7   Fare.   1/7

2863 21   21 2863

115. Midhurst trains used the up bay, until passenger services ceased in 1935. Selsey trains used an independent station to the south of the main station. (Lens of Sutton)

114. Sister I3 no. 2083 runs onto Stockbridge Road crossing whilst the last coach is still on Basin Road crossing. This undated photograph was probably taken around 1939, the GWR coaches being the Brighton portion of the Cardiff train. (Lens of Sutton)

116. The first main line electric locomotive on the Southern Railway was built in 1942 and numbered CC1, the CC indicating two sets of three driving axles. It is pictured here when five years old. On the left is a mirror to assist the signalman opening the gates, and in the distance the locomotive water tower, which survived the steam age until June 1983. (C.R.L. Coles)

118. Class E4 no. 32503 leaves Chichester with a solitary utility van in February 1961, the relatively new brick building being the Southdown bus station. Over 70 of these successful engines were built at Brighton between 1897 and 1903 but only one survives – *Birch Grove*, on the Bluebell Railway. (P. Hay)

117. West Country class no. 34048 *Crediton* is seen leaving for Brighton with the through train from Plymouth in May 1953. Ahead of the locomotive is the rubble of the former police station. The then newly constructed County Court is in the background. (C.R.L. Coles)

119. The gasworks, although only over the road from the goods yard, surprisingly never had a rail connection. Here we see the 11 a.m. from Brighton leaving Chichester at 11.52 on 11th June 1962, with arrival at Cardiff ex-pected at 4.35 p.m. No. 34057 was one of the Battle of Britain class and was named after one of the airfields – *Biggin Hill* – a name now carried by a locomotive on the Severn Valley Railway. (S.C. Nash)

120. A fast Brighton to Portsmouth Harbour train runs in, during August 1980, past the gasworks site, with closed circuit TV cameras on the right hand tower and floodlights for them, on the left. The line is nearly 150 years old and this picture shows some of the latest technology to come into the fascinating story of continuous improvement on this interest-ing part of Coastway West. (D. Dornom)